THE WORD
TOOK FLESH

THE WORD TOOK FLESH

INCARNATING THE CHRISTIAN MESSAGE IN IGBO LAND OF NIGERIA IN THE LIGHT OF VATICAN II'S THEOLOGY OF INCULTURATION.

Hyacinth Kalu

iUniverse, Inc.
Bloomington

THE WORD TOOK FLESH
INCARNATING THE CHRISTIAN MESSAGE IN IGBO LAND
OF NIGERIA IN THE LIGHT OF VATICAN II'S THEOLOGY OF
INCULTURATION.

iUniverse books may be ordered through booksellers or by contacting:

iUniverse
1663 Liberty Drive
Bloomington, IN 47403
www.iuniverse.com
1-800-Authors (1-800-288-4677)

ISBN: 978-1-4620-2540-4 (sc)
ISBN: 978-1-4620-2772-9 (ebk)

Library of Congress Control Number: 2011909020

Printed in the United States of America

iUniverse rev. date: 06/06/2011

TABLE OF CONTENTS

To my brothers who are my pillars of support

Introduction

Christianity from its inception has been a missionary religion; a religion that keeps faithfully the *mandatum magnum* of her Lord and founder, Jesus Christ, who says "Go therefore and make disciples of all nations." (Matt. 28: 18)[1] Expressing this belief, the Second Vatican Council (Vatican II) said:

> The Church has an obligation to proclaim the faith and salvation which comes from Christ, both by reason of the express command which the order of bishops inherited from the apostles, an obligation in the discharge of which they are assisted by priests, and one which they share with the successor of St. Peter, the supreme pastor of the church, and also by reason of the life which Christ infuses into his members.[2]

In exercising this mandate, the Church through the ages has always seen her mission as one that cuts across, mingles, and transcends cultures. The Christian Church understands herself as having a universal vocation to touch and evangelize the human

---

[1] All biblical references in this work are taken from the standard edition of *The Jerusalem Bible* (London: Darton, Longman and Todd, Ltd., 1966.)

[2] Decree on the Church's Missionary Activity—*Ad Gentes Divinitus.* December 7, 1965, n.5.

race irrespective of culture, tribe, language, ethnicity, and nationality. Inspired by this vision, the Christian message was brought into Nigeria for the first time in the late 15ᵗʰ century and early 16ᵗʰ century through the Catholic Portuguese missionaries. This effort was short lived. A vibrant and lasting Christianity eventually came to Nigeria in general and Igbo land in particular in the 1800s.

In this work, my aim and concern is not to trace the historical origin and development of Christianity in Igbo land, but to see how far the message has taken root in Igbo culture. If the message was successfully inculturated, what factors were responsible? If it was not, what hindered it? Again, the next question will be: what can the Church do, looking at the exigencies of today's Igbo society, to make the gospel message more relevant in the life of the Igbo people? Some scholars say that the only way out is INCULTURATION. This answer raises other questions: what do we mean by inculturation? Can the Christian message mingle or mix well with Igbo culture? If yes, what are the principles and what prospect does it hold both to the Church and to the Igbo people? If no, what are the obstacles and challenges?

In addressing these questions, the objective of this work is to find and propose ways of incorporating the Christian message into the life of the Igbo person so that he/she can be at home with the message of the gospel, and at the same time a true Igbo at home with the Igbo culture. In other words, the aim is to assist the Igbo person to truly live out his/her Christian life as a truly Igbo person, and not an Igbo in 'foreign garments'.

As the title suggests, the work is concerned with the inculturation of the Christian message in Igbo land following the principles enunciated especially by Vatican II, and in other official Church documents prior and post Vatican II. This topic is treated against the general background of contact between religions and cultures. It will examine the co-mingling of the Christian religion with African traditional religion, especially as practiced in Igbo land of Nigeria. It is not within the scope of this work to treat the origin of Christianity and her missionary activities in the whole of African and Nigeria.

Thus, the central focus of this work is the contact between Christianity and Igbo traditional culture and religious life. Attention is focused primarily on the Roman Catholic Church. Hence, when we talk about the Church in this work, we are referring to the Catholic Church. However, occasional mentions will also be made of other Christian denominations within Igbo land in their relationships and attitudes towards the cultural and traditional practices of the Igbo people.

Furthermore, the title of this book suggests theological and religio-cultural issues. Consequently, in addressing these issues, I will be drawing from the official documents of the Church, especially the Documents of the Second Vatican Council, Papal encyclicals, and the teachings of the magisterium regarding Church and culture. These documents will provide us with the theological basis and principles of inculturation. The works of some eminent theologians will also be consulted and drawn from to balance our arguments. Most importantly, this work will draw largely from the rich works and researches of African and Nigerian scholars of African traditional religion and culture. The importance of these works and researches is that they are borne out of thorough field works and practical experiences.

A greater input in this work is based on my personal and practical experience on the subject. As a priest for many years, and as one born and raised in a traditional village and religio-cultural setting, I have been exposed to many Christians struggling to reconcile their faith with their cultural beliefs. All through my priestly ministry in Nigeria, I worked in communities where native culture and tradition are still very strong and exercise overwhelming influences on Christians within the community. I have also, in some occasions, mediated in conflicts involving Christians and followers of (Igbo) African traditional religion over matters of faith, worship and culture. I have equally been a victim of attack on issues of Christians being Christians and at same time true Igbos, faithful their cultural and traditional heritage. This wealth of experience will be employed in this work.

To put this work in its proper context, it has been divided into five chapters. Chapter one explains who the Igbo people are. It also gives us a working definition of the key terms in this work, namely: culture and inculturation. Chapter two is on the Church and her mission of evangelizing cultures and the inculturation of the Christian message in these cultures. It also discusses in general terms how the missionaries carried on and imposed Christianity, laden with western imperialism and biases, in mission lands. Using the Igbo people as a study of the success and failure of inculturation, chapter three gives us the idea of the life, religion and culture of the Igbo people before the advent of Christianity, and how much they were affected positively and/or negatively with the coming of Christianity. How the missionaries look at the Igbo people and their culture will also be discussed in this chapter. It will conclude with a look at the problems of inculturating the Christian message in Igbo land, especially as it touches on western biases. Chapter four of this work is on the possibilities and dangers of inculturating the Christian message into the Igbo culture. In this chapter, we will propose a thought experiment in the process of inculturation in Igbo land. Finally, chapter five will look at the prospects and challenges of incarnating (the taking flesh of the divine Message of Christ in human culture), the Christian message in Igbo land. This chapter will end with a re-appraisal of the whole work.

Chapter One

BASIC FOUNDATIONS

1.1 THE IGBO LAND OF NIGERIA: PEOPLE, RELIGION, AND CULTURE.

The Igbo Land, which forms the South-East Geopolitical zone of Nigeria, is inhabited by the Igbo ethnic group, one of the largest and dominant tribes in Nigeria. Sharing geographical boundaries with "Ibibio to the east, Ijaw and Agbor to the southwest, and Idoma to the north, Igbo land occupies an area of 40,922 Sq. Km."[3] This territory "lies between 5° and 7° north of the Equator and between the 6° and 8° east of the Greenwich meridian, spanning the river Niger approximately midway between the Niger-Benue confluence to the North and the Atlantic to the South."[4]

Ethnologically, the Igbo people are seen as an ancient race. Historically, the Igbo people are believed to have a civilization

---

[3]   Raphael Chijioke, *African Cultural Values: Igbo Political Leadership in Colonial Nigeria, 1900-1966.* (New York: Routedge, 2006), 5.

[4]   C.O. Obiego, *African Image of the Ultimate Reality: Analysis of Igbo Ideas of Life and Death in Relation to Chukwu.* (Berlin: Peter Lang, 1984), 32.

5

spanning nearly 8,000 years.[5] Many accounts attest to the fact the Igbo had settled in what is today known as Nigeria by "the third millennium BC (3000 BC)."[6] Tracing this long span of history, Udeani divides the history of the Igbos into three periods: the pre-agricultural period, the agricultural period, and the period of agriculture and commerce.[7]

Many hypotheses abound regarding the origin of the Igbos. Some scholars trace it back to the Biblical Jews. This hypothesis sees the Igbos as one of the lost tribes of Israel, descending from Gad through Eri (one of the sons of Gad) who settled at Nri, a Kingdom said to be the earliest Igbo state, which emerged in 900 AD and lasted for over a thousand years.[8] Proponents of this hypothesis support their views drawing from the rich religio-cultural similarities between the traditional Jews and Igbo people. According G. T. Basden, a European anthropologist, as cited by Afigbo, "The investigator cannot help being struck with the similitude between them (Igbo practices) and some of the ideas and practices of the [Hebrew] Levitical code."[9]

In another vein, some ethnographers have traced the origin to the Igbo to Egypt. According to Afigbo, M.D.V. Jeffreys said emphatically, "Egypt held the key to Igbo origin and history."[10]

---

5   David Asonye Ihenacho, *African Christianity Rises: A Critical Study of the Catholicism of the Igbo People of Nigeria, Vol I.* (New York: iUniverse, Inc., 2004), 1.

6   Adiele E. Afigbo, *An Outline of Igbo History.* (Owerri, Nigeria: RADA, 1986), 1.

7   Chibueze Udeani, *Inculturation as Dialogue. Igbo Culture and the Message of Christ.* (Amsterdam: Rodopi, 2007), 14-16

8   Odumegwu Ojukwu, "Igbos: Are they Jews?" *Nigerian Tribune*, May 18, 2007. http://www.tribune.com.ng/18052007/igbo_feat.html (accessed March 20, 2009)

9   Adiele E. Afigbo *Ropes in the Sand: Studies in Igbo History and Culture.* (Nsukka: University of Nigeria, 1981), 18.

10   Afigbo *Ropes in the Sand*, 6.

He arrived at his conclusion because of what he considers as a dual division of Igbo social structure, and the *Ichi* facial marks and other interesting features of Igbo traditional religion he believed must have been learned from Egypt.[11]

Many indigenous archeologists and anthropologists today have gone far beyond these generalists' claims on Igbo origin to favor a theory of non-migration in studying the history of the Igbo. Anthropologists at the University of Benin, Nigeria, have uncovered fossils of a proto-Igbo civilization—Ugwelle Okigwe stone civilization dating about 6,000 BC. This archeological discovery traces other pockets of civilization in Igbo land such as Afikpo, Nsukka metal civilization (3000 BC), and Owerrri, Ika, Ndosimili-Ukwani, and Ngwa (8-18 AD).[12] Affirming these findings, Elizabeth Isichei observed that ethnographic, archeological, and ecological evidences have shown that:

> The first cradles of human habitation in the Igbo area were probably the Cross River and the Anambra Valley—Nsukka escarpment. In each of these areas, later Stone Age sites have been excavated. A rock shelter at Afikpo was first inhabited about five thousand years age, by people who made rough red pottery and a variety of Stone tools. . . . Excavations at the University of Nigeria Nsukka, uncovered the pottery, 4500 years old, and Ibagwa, a town in Nsukka area, has a rock shelter which yielded both ancient pottery and tools of stone.[13]

However, even in the prevailing theories of non-migration, there are usually some allowances made of short-distance migrations and movements within southern regions of the

[11]   Ibid.

[12]   Ihenacho, *African Christianity Rises*, 7.

[13]   Elizabeth Isichei, *A History of the Igbo People* (London: Macmillan Press, 1976), 3.

present-day Igbo nation. It is generally accepted that the first people who inhabited this area came from the area of the Niger-Benue confluence. As Afigbo explained:

> On leaving the general area of the Niger-Benue confluence the early Igbo people would appear to have spread along the Nsukka-Okigwe highlands which at the time constituted the most habitable parts of what later became Eastern Nigeria. The Southward movement of this early Igbo people along this cuesta continued for centuries as more and more people came in from the north and as the first migrants multiplied. This led to the vanguard of the movement being pushed beyond the southern tip of the Nsukka-Udi cuesta into the rolling plains to the south where they multiplied. These groups became the Uratta, Ikwere, Etche, Asa and Ndoki Igbo of present times.[14]

Traditional Igbo society can be described as a homogeneous society; a society where religion enfolds the whole of life. Culture is understood from the religious perspective. As Ejizu puts it, "Religion is the womb of culture in the traditional Igbo background. It permeates most aspects of life, and infuses them with meaning and significance."[15] Social life is regulated by the dictates and principles of religion, and there is no dividing line between the religion, ethics and morality. As a matter of fact,

"The gods serve as policemen"[16] in matters relating to the ordering of society and people's life. Accordingly, "Among the Igbo, religion and law are so closely interwoven that many of the

---

[14]   Afigbo, *An Outline of Igbo History*. 3.

[15]   Christopher Ejizu, *The Influence of African Indigenous Religions on Roman Catholicism, The Igbo Example.* http://www.afrikaworld. net/afrel/ejizu-atrcath.htm (accessed May 18, 2008).

[16]   Christopher Ejizu, *Ofo, Igbo Ritual Symbol._*(Enugu: Fourth Dimension Publishers, Ltd, 1986), 90.

powerful legal sanctions are derived directly from the gods."[17] For the Igbos, a completely secular world does not exist. Everybody is religious and everything is done religiously. The inseparability of religion and the totality of the Igbo people's whole of existence are summarized by a down to earth observation by Major A. G. Leonard, a pioneer British colonial master to Igbo land. In his words,

> They [the Igbos] are in the strict and natural sense of the word, a truly and deeply religious people, of whom it can be said, as it has been said of the Hindus, that they eat religiously, drink religiously, bathe religiously, dress religiously, and sin religiously. In few words, the religion of these natives, as I have endeavored to point out is their existence, and their existence is their religion.[18]

Expressing this connection and relationship in the words of Udeani,

> The Igbo people, [traditionally and religiously] live in two forms of time, sacred and profane; of which the more important from is the sacred time. This entails the paradoxical aspect of a circular, reversible time which could be re-enacted or re-lived. It presents a mythical form of the eternal now, in which religious people immerse themselves through periodic rites. As regards profane time, the [Igbo] religious person sees a connection between this and the sacred time. The profane time, in which human existence and historical events take place, is made possible through the sacred time, the eternal now mythical event.[19]

---

[17]   Arthur G. Leonard, *The Lower Niger and its Tribes*. (London: Frank Cass, 1906), 30

[18]   Ibid, 429.

[19]   Udeani, *Inculturation as Dialogue*, 29

As Eliade would put it, "it is the holy, mythical time which justifies as an exemplary model existential historical time. For religious people profane time is sustained through turning to holy, non-historical time by means of rites."[20]

Presently, the geographical territory of Igbo land is the south-eastern zone of Nigeria comprising Abia, Anambra, Ebonyi, Enugu, and Imo States of Nigeria. Prominent cities in Igbo land today include Onitsha, Asaba, Enugu, Nsukka, Abakaliki, Awka, Nnewi Amaigo, Obigbo, Nri, Owerri, Orlu, Okigwe, Mbaise, Umuahia, Bende, Afikpo, Ohafia, Abam, Ihechiowa, and Arochukwu. The language of the Igbo people is *Igbo*, which belongs to the "*KWA* sub-group of the Niger-Congo language groups."[21]

The population of the Igbo People is 19,119,607 as per the 2006 national census, representing 18% of Nigeria's population.[22] Relying on population increase since 2006, the population is probably above 20 million putting it "among the most populous single indigenous groups in sub-Sahara Africa."[23]

1.2 CULTURE: WHAT IS IT?

Before speaking of the Igbo culture, it is vital to explore what we mean by the word "culture." The term culture has been variously defined and understood by many scholars, each from the viewpoint of his or her own field of scholarship. Etymologically, the term culture is derived

> From the Latin *colere* meaning 'to till or cultivate'. The term is sometimes used to include all of the creative

---

[20] Mircea Eliade, *The Sacred and The Profane: The Nature of Religion.* (San Diego: Harcourt Inc., 1987), 70-71.

[21] Ihenacho, *African Christianity Rises*, 7.

[22] Paden, *Faith and Politics in Nigeria*, 6

[23] Christopher Ejizu, "The Traditional Igbo Perception of Reality: Its Dialectics and Dilemma," in *Bigard Theological Studies*, Vol. 9 (Enugu, Nigeria: 1989), 58-73.

expressions of man in all fields of human endeavor. At other times it is confined to creative expression in the areas of the liberal arts. In the second of these senses the term is sometimes extended to personal cultivation.[24]

It is generally believed that culture is the way a particular people behave, act and live. In other words, it is a way of life. It is humans that define culture, without humans, there is no culture. Expressed in another way, culture is the totality of patterns according to which human beings think, act and feel. It is the channel through which people view the whole of their experience. Accordingly, Niebuhr said, "Culture is the work of men's minds and hands. It is that portion of man's heritage in any place and time which has been given us designedly and laboriously by other men, not what has come to us via the mediation of nonhuman beings."[25]

One of the most celebrated definitions of culture is that given by the renowned sociologist, Edward Tylor. He defined culture as "that complex whole which includes knowledge, belief, art, morals, laws, customs and any other capabilities and habits acquired by man as a member of society."[26] It is clear from this definition that culture evolves and thrives within the society. Society creates culture and culture on the other hand shapes society. Culture has a social character. It is not an individual thing. Individuals experience and transmit culture uniquely, but culture transcends individual experiences. Individuals within a culture share an interactive, learned perspective on appropriate social behavior. Here culture includes the behavioral pattern of individuals within the society. In the words of Niebuhr:

---

[24] William Reese, *Dictionary of Philosophy and Religion*. (New York: Humanity Books, 1999), 151.

[25] H. Richard Niebuhr, *Christ and Culture*. (New York: Harper and Row, 1951), 33.

[26] Edward B. Tylor, *Primitive Culture*. (New York: J.P. Putnam & sons, 1920), 1.

> Individuals may use culture in their own ways; they
> may change elements in their culture, yet what they
> use and change is social. Culture is the social heritage
> they (individuals within society) receive and transmit.
> Whatever is purely private, so that it neither derives
> from nor enters into social life is not a part of culture.
> Conversely, social life is always cultural.[27]

Based on this understanding, Niebuhr went ahead to define
culture as that which "includes speech, education, tradition, myth,
science, art, philosophy, government, law, rite, belief, inventions,
technologies."[28]

As a people's way of life, culture, therefore, "Explicitly and
implicitly teaches its members how to organize their experience.
To learn a culture is to learn how to perceive, judge, and act in
ways that are recognizable, predictable, and understandable to
others in the same community."[29]

> Culture is not simply about behavior. It is also about ideas.
> The mental basis of culture is commonly stressed in modern
> definitions of culture. For example, Clifford Geertz defines
> culture as, "A system of inherited conceptions expressed
> in symbolic forms by means of which human beings
> communicate, perpetuate and develop their knowledge
> about, and their attitudes towards life."[30]

In the traditional society, there is a very close connection
between religion and culture. For instance, in the African

---

[27]   Niebuhr, *Christ and Culture*, 33.

[28]   Ibid.

[29]   Duane E. Campbell, *Choosing Democracy: A practical guide to
       Multicultural Education, 3rd* Ed. (New Jersey: Prentice Hall, 2004), 43.

[30]   Clifford Geertz, *The Interpretation of Culture*. (New York: Basic
       Books, 1975), 89

traditional religion, the cultural life of the people is expressed in their religious beliefs and practices. The norms, patterns of behavior, and the worldview are connected with the religion of the people. Social norms are enforced through religious taboos. In his attempt to portray the connection between religion and culture and how they can impact each other, Aylward Shorter said:

> Culture is essentially a transmitted pattern of meanings embodied in symbols, a pattern capable of development and change, and it belongs to the concept of humanness itself. It follows that, if religion is a human phenomenon or human activity, it must affect, and be affected by, culture.[31]

All the above definitions and interpretations of culture are synthesized and given a broader meaning and application by the Second Vatican Council. In the *Pastoral Constitution on the Church in the Modern World, Gaudium et Spes,* the Council stated:

> Man comes to a true and full humanity only through culture, which is through the cultivation of the goods and values of nature. Wherever human life is involved, therefore, nature and culture are quite intimately connected one with the other. The word "culture" in its general sense indicates everything whereby man develops and perfects his many bodily and spiritual qualities; . . . Thence it follows that human culture has necessarily a historical and social aspect and the word "culture" also often assumes a sociological and ethnological sense. According to this sense we speak of a plurality of cultures. Different styles of life and multiple scales of values arise from the diverse manner of using things, of laboring, of expressing oneself, of practicing religion,

---

[31] Aylward Shorter, *Towards a Theology of Inculturation.* (New York: Orbis Books, 1997), 5.

of forming customs, of establishing laws and juridic institutions, of cultivating the sciences, the arts and beauty. Thus the customs handed down to it form the patrimony proper to each human community. It is also in this way that there is formed the definite, historical milieu which enfolds the man of every nation and age and from which he draws the values which permit him to promote civilization. [32]

This broad and well articulated definition and explanation of culture by Vatican II heavily influenced the Council's formulation of the theology of inculturation.

Based on our understanding of culture, it means that a proper evangelization and an effective incarnation[33] of the Christian message in Igbo land cannot be effectively realized outside the Igbo cultural context. Hence, the necessity of inculturation.

1.3 INCULTURATION: MEANING AND CONCEPT.

The term Inculturation, as a word, may not sound familiar to theologians and scholars prior to Vatican II. It is quite a new term that emerges in an attempt to understand the mission of the Church in relation to all the cultures of the world. However, the term may be new, but the concept and what it stands for is not all new in the Church's evangelizing mission. According to Oliver Onwubiko:

> Inculturation, therefore, is a new vision of an old problem in the Church or a new approach to a solution of an old

---

[32] Vatican II, *Gaudiun et Spes*, no. 53.

[33] Incarnation is the coming together or the union of the divine nature and the human nature in the person of Jesus Christ. By taking flesh, Jesus brought these two distinct natures into one. Within the context of this work, incarnation refers to the union or coming together of faith (the divine message of Christ) and human culture. That is faith taking flesh in human culture.

problem, or still a new interpretation of an old solution
of the Church and culture encounter. It came into use
after the Second Vatican Council. The term itself does
not appear in the documents of the Council. Authors
use it in relation to: "Inculturation of the Church",
"Inculturation of Christianity", "Inculturation of the
Gospel Message", and "Inculturation of the Faith", all
expressing the same objective and finality.[34]

Since the emergence of the term into the Church's missionary theology,
there are terms which are either used with or are interchanged, or even
confused with it. Such terms, among others, are enculturation and
acculturation. Explaining what these terms mean will assist us to properly
get a clear picture of the meaning and concept of inculturation.

Some theologians and scholars use the term enculturation
in expressing the concept of integration and/or incarnating the
Christian message in a particular culture. This is not an adequate
concept. Enculturation is the imbibing or adaptation into a
culture or cultural system within one's society, or a culture other
than one's culture when one finds himself of herself in a new
society or sphere of life. In the words of Aylward Shorter,

> Enculturation refers to the cultural learning process of the
> individual, the process by which a person is inserted into his
> culture. It is a concept closely related to that of socialization
> of an individual by society. While the process obviously
> includes formal teaching and learning; it is very largely an
> informal, and even an unconscious experience.[35]

Inculturation on the other hand is purely a conscious process,
which may and at times do involve a process of dialogue. It is not

---

[34] Oliver A. Onwubiko, *Theory and Practice of Inculturation: An
African Perspective*. (Enugu: Snaap Press, 1992), 1.

[35] Shorter, *Towards a Theology of Inculturation*, 5.

an insertion of a person into a culture, but rather "the interaction of faith and culture."[36]

Another term that is confused and/ or interchanged with inculturation is acculturation. Acculturation is a purely sociological concept and not a theological concept. While inculturation may include sociological elements, it is above all a theological concept.[37] As a sociological concept, acculturation has to do with an interaction or integration of two different cultures. This interaction need not involve a religious faith interacting with a particular culture. Whereas inculturation as a theological concept must of necessity involve the interaction of a religious faith and an indigenous culture. In our context, inculturation has to do with faith related matters. Faith, especially the Christian faith, though can be practiced in a particular culture, is not identical with any particular culture. Defining acculturation, Shorter said:

> By acculturation is meant the encounter between one culture and another or the encounter between different cultures. This is perhaps the principal cause of cultural change. It is a process which is a necessary concomitant of culture itself. Human beings possess the collective freedom to modify their particular cultural traditions through contact with people of other cultures. Culture itself comes into existence through collective processes, and the encounter between cultures is likewise a collective process largely beyond the scope of individual choice. It

---

[36] Ibid., 4

[37] Sociology analyzes the patterns and meanings of human interaction within specific social, cultural, and temporal contexts. It does not raise theistic or doctrinal questions. Theology on the other hand deals with theistic and doctrinal issues in an attempt to interpret the signs and symbols of salvation experience so as to develop a meaningful and coherent moral narrative that informs and guides believers.

is, of course, an encounter between two different sets of symbols and conceptions, two different interpretations of experience, two different social identities. Unreflective and unprogrammed though it may be, the encounter is fraught with complexity. Its consequences can be discerned *post factum* at the conscious level, but many of the conflicts it engenders are worked out at the subconscious level.[38]

This is exactly what most of the early missionaries who came to African in general and to Nigeria and Igbo land in particular practiced. They implanted the Christian message through the process of acculturating the African and the Igbo people into the European culture, without inculturating the Christian message into the culture and life of the people.

Having made these distinctions, the next question that necessarily arises is: what, then, is inculturation. There is an inextricable connection between culture and inculturation. Although, inculturation is a theological concept that has to do with the practice of faith, it is faith as practice within a particular cultural and social context. In line with this understanding, Aylward Shorter said:

> Culture refers to the way of life of a people, to the ideas and images that orientate its thoughts and behavior. Inculturation refers to the Christian renewal of culture, the transforming dialogue of culture with the Gospel, and indeed the person of Jesus Christ. Inculturation can therefore be correctly called a way of life in itself, since this dialogue and this transformation have to be experienced and lived by people. It is lived and experienced primarily by people in community and especially in the basic communities which are the hub of social and cultural life.[39]

---

[38] Ibid., 7.
[39] Ibid., 268.

17

Inculturation simply put is a dialogue between faith and culture. This dialogue presupposes not an imposition of one upon the other but a two-way activity of give and take; that is faith taking from culture and culture enriched by faith. This is a very vital element of inculturation, because while the Church is set to enrich and evangelize culture, she in turn must realize that there are things she must learn and take from the culture of the people. For example, the Church must understand, at least, the people's worldview as expressed in their culture, and not ignorantly condemn whatever that does not fit into her pattern. When the people see the willingness and openness of the Church to learn and take from their culture, they in turn will be willing to listen to what the Church is offering them. Understood thus, inculturation would mean the presentation and expression of the Christian message in forms proper, and not foreign, to a particular culture. This means that the language and terms of inculturation in its practical application will necessarily vary from one culture to another while the principle itself remains the same.

By way of definition, therefore, inculturation "is the creative and dynamic relationship between the Christian message and a culture or cultures."[40] For this creativity and dynamism to be an inculturation it must:

> Be understood as the honest, serious and critical attempt to enable the Message of Christ to be understood by peoples of every culture, locality and age. Stretched further, this means understanding the Message of Christ within the very world and thought patterns of the many peoples. It is the continuous endeavor at making the message of Christ at home in the cultures of each people."[41]

---

[40] Ibid., 11.

[41] Udeani, *Inculturation as Dialogue*, viii.

Furthermore, citing Fr. Pedro Arrup, Peter Schineller, has this to say by way of defining inculturation:

> Inculturation is the incarnation of Christian life and of the Christian message in a particular culture, in such a way that this experience not only finds expression through elements proper to the culture in question, but becomes a principle that animates, directs and unifies the culture, transforming and remaking it so as to bring about "a new creation."[42]

Inculturation, as a way incarnating the Christian message in a particular culture, begins with a particular local Church but does not end there. It must have a universal dimension; that is, enriching the ecclesial communion of the universal church. The inculturated Church within a particular culture does not become a new and distinct Church, but a Church renewed and recreated through a genuine interaction and dialogue between the Gospel and the local culture, in such a way the one faith centered in the person of Jesus Christ is now experienced and celebrated in a manner peculiar to that culture. This is the view that Roest Crollius expressed in his definition of inculturation as,

> The integration of the Christian experience of a local Church into the culture of its people in such a way that this experience not only expresses itself in elements of this culture so as to create a new unity and communion, not only within the culture in question but also as an enrichment of the Church universal.[43]

---

[42] Peter Schineller, *A Handbook on Inculturation*. (New York: Paulist Press, 1990), 6.

[43] Nathaniel I. Ndiokwere, *The African Church, Today and Tomorrow*, vol. II. (Enugu: Snaap Press, 1994), 32.

Expanding on Crollius' definition, Ndiokwere explained that inculturation implies,

> The activity of the Church, at a particular place in time, to present and live the Christian message **faithfully** in language, signs and symbols and actions which speaks to the people in so convincing a way that they naturally and readily identify with it and whole-heartedly participate in it and contribute to it. . . . It is God's self-revelation from a people's cultural perspective, tradition and life and the same people responding from the same perspective.[44]

Looking at inculturation strictly from an African perspective, Udeani has this to say:

> In terms of African inculturation theology, the movement . . . involves a wholesome encounter of African traditional religion and culture with the Christian message as opposed to a mere selection of themes therefrom. This avoids the functionalization and instrumentalization of the African culture. African culture is treated as a whole in itself. The encounter is between the African culture and the original sources of Christian faith. African traditional religion is even looked at for insights of orientation and pattern in theologizing. African traditional religion, being a way of life rather than a collection of doctrines makes it easier for the African inculturation theology to be more practical-life-oriented in contrast to the cognitive-knowledge-oriented Western theology.[45]

The concept of inculturation as seen above provides a working tool for this work, and also corrects some of the deficiencies of

---

[44]   Ibid, 31.
[45]   Udeani, *Inculturation as Dialogue,* 136.

the adaptation, enculturation and acculturation approaches. The inculturation approach thus understood has no element of missionary paternalism. African culture in general and Igbo culture in particular is fully recognized, not only when it has something which, according to the judgment of Western theology, can be fixed into the Western Christianity. It is recognized for its own sake, on its own worth, for its own thought patterns, religiosity, liveliness and ability to contribute in making the people better Christians as well as in its ability to master the future.

Chapter Two

THE CHURCH AND CULTURE

2.1 CHRIST AND CULTURE.

At the center of the Christian message is Jesus Christ. As St. Paul said, " . . . we are preaching a crucified Christ; to the Jews an obstacle that they cannot get over, to the pagans madness, but to those who have been called, whether they are Jews or Greeks, a Christ who is the power and wisdom of God." (I Cor. 2:23-24).[46] It is this preaching of Christ and his word that produces faith. (cf. Rom. 10:17).

However, who is this Jesus Christ? The Jesus that is preached is not just a Cosmic Jesus or a Celestial Jesus, but a Jesus who was born within the context of a particular culture, who grew within this culture and who expressed and communicated his message within the cultural milieu. Put in the words of Shorter, "There could have been no earthly ministry for Jesus if he had not adopted the cultural concepts, symbols and behavior of his hearers. His cultural solidarity with the Palestinian communities of his day was a necessary condition for communication with

---

[46] All biblical references in this work are taken from the standard edition of *The Jerusalem Bible* (London: Darton, Longman and Todd, Ltd., 1966)

them."[47] In this Jesus, the divine and human came together. Put in another way, faith and culture came together. Thus, by becoming human, God in Christ identified himself with culture. As St. John expressed, "In the beginning was the Word: the Word was with God and the Word was God. . . . The Word took flesh and dwelt among us." (John 1:1,14). This Eternal Word, Jesus Christ, was human in everything except sin.[48] (cf. Heb. 4:15) This essential co-mingling of the divine and the human is what is called the mystery of the incarnation. As explained by Eileen Flynn and Gloria Thomas, "The dogma of the incarnation is very simply the coming together of God and humanity in Jesus. Jesus' humanity is the unique response to divinity, a place where God's self-communication is fully received."[49]

Pointing out the inextricable relationship between Jesus and culture, Peter Schineller said:

> The most directly theological word to express the meaning of inculturation is incarnation. "The Word became flesh and dwelt among us" (Jn 1: 14) . . . The Son of God, conceived by the power of the Spirit, is born of Mary. Incarnation refers to the entire Christ-event—the coming, birth, growth, daily life and struggle, teaching, healing, resting, celebrating, suffering, dying, and rising of Jesus Christ. . . . Jesus was born, lived and died in a particular context or culture. He learned the language and customs, and in and through these he expressed the truth and love of God. He did not consciously indigenize

---

47   Aylward Shorter, *Towards a Theology of Inculturation.* (New York: Orbis Books, 1997), 80.

48   Sin, is understood as an offence against God—by any thought, word, deed or omission against the law of God. Cf. Francis Ripley, *This is the Faith.* (Illinois: Tan Books, 2002), 53.

49   Eileen Flynn and Gloria Thomas, *Living Faith: An Introduction to Theology,* 2nd Ed. (Kansas City: Sheed and Ward, 1989), 58.

or inculturate, but instinctively took part fully in the culture he was born into, and then critically affirmed and challenged that culture in the light of the spirit.[50]

Jesus himself is, therefore, in relationship to culture. In a classic study, McBrien, drawing from the Protestant theologian H. Richard Niebuhr, identifies five such relationships, namely, Christ *against* culture (He challenges the culture of his time) and Christ *of* culture (He was born and he grew up as a first-century Jew from Galilee). The other relationships are, Christ *above* culture (He was not tied to cultural situation of his time, but rather lived above it by his life style and example); Christ and culture in *paradox* (His life style and teaching was seen as making a paradigm shift from the status quo. This explains why he often conflicted with the Jews, and he was eventually killed because of this paradox); and Christ as the *transformer* of culture ('Full of grace and truth' Jon 1: 14, he injected new life and new attitude into the culture of his time)[51]

Stressing on Christ as the transformer of culture, a position, which St. Augustine promoted in his theology, and which I find most appealing among the five relationships of Christ and culture, Niebuhr said, "Christ is the transformer of culture in the sense that he redirects, reinvigorates, and regenerates that life of man, expressed in all human works."[52]

As a man of culture, Christ is therefore, primarily the subject matter of inculturation. There is no inculturation so to speak that ignores the historical Jesus as a cultural person. The realization of this fact has shaped a better understanding and appreciation

---

50   Peter Schineller, *A Handbook on Inculturation*. (New York: Paulist Press, 1990), 20.

51   Richard P. McBrien, *Catholicism*. (New York: HarperCollins Publishers, 1994), 406.

52   H. Richard Niebuhr, *Christ and Culture*. (New York: Harper and Row, 1951), 209

of Christ and his message in various cultures of the world. As Niebuhr explained:

> In every culture to which the Gospel comes there are men who hail Jesus as the Messiah of their society, the fulfiller of its hopes and aspirations, the perfector of its faith, the source of its holiest spirit . . . On the one hand they interpret culture through Christ, regarding those elements in it as most important which are most accordant with his work and person; on the other hand they understand Christ through culture, selecting from his teaching and action as well as from Christian doctrine about him such points as seem to agree with what is best in civilization. So they harmonize Christ and culture.[53]

Expressing the same view as Niebuhr, Aylward Shorter said:

> A good example of inculturation is provided by the successive images of Jesus through the centuries, as the tradition of faith passed from Judaism into the Greco-Roman culture of the Mediterranean, thence into the Christian Roman Empire, Byzantium, the Middle Ages of western Europe, the Renaissance, Reformation and Counter-Reformation, the Age of Enlightenment, the Romantic movement, the non-western experience of decolonization and liberation and so on. Jesus was depicted successively as Lord of History, Light of the Gentiles, King of Kings, True Icon of God, the Crucified God, the Bridegroom of the Soul, the Universal Man, the Mirror of Truth, the Prince of Peace, the Poet of the Soul, the Liberator, the Ancestor, Master of Initiation, Healer and many more. All of these images correspond to particular cultures, places and epochs, but all are in

---

53   Ibid, 83-84.

the authentic tradition concerning Jesus. All these images can be indexed back to the outlooks, and sometimes even to the very words, of the New Testament itself. They are an extraordinary example of the "marriage of meanings" that is the essence of inculturation.[54]

In his life, person and ministry, Jesus gives meaning to cultures. He shows us that culture *per se* is not diabolical or derogatory. He shows that in every culture, there is already a seed of the Gospel implanted by God himself who took human nature within a cultural context so that man in his culture background may share in God's divine nature.

2.2 THE CHURCH: MEANING AND CONCEPT.

Inculturation as a dialogue between faith and culture is essentially a dialogue between the Church and culture. The Church carries out the mission of incarnating the message of Christ into various cultures of the world. However, the question here is: what is the Church, who is the Church, how does she come to be, and how does she relate to the world and its cultures?

To have a clear picture of the meaning and concept of the Church, we shall first look at the root of the word—church. Etymologically:

The term *church* (Anglo-Saxon, *cirice, circe*; Modern German, *Kirche;* Sweden, *Kyrka*) is the name employed in the Teutonic languages to render the Greek *ekklesia* (*ecclesia*), the term by which the New Testament writers denote the society founded by Our Lord Jesus Christ. The derivation of the word has been much debated. It is now agreed that it is derived from the Greek *kyriakon*

---

54 Aylward Shorter, *Inculturation of African Traditional Religious Values in Christianity—How Far?* http://www.afrikaworld.net/afrel/shorter.htm (accessed May 12, 2008)

(*cyriacon*), i.e. the Lord's house, a term that from the third century was used, as well as *ekklesia*, to signify a Christian place of worship.[55]

The term *ekklesia* is not a third century invention; its usage also goes beyond just a place of Christian worship, it extends to those who gather in such place of worship. Discussing the term *ekklesia*, Hans Küng said:

> In secular Greek usage, *ekklesia* means the assembly, the political gathering of the people. But the model of the New Testament concept of *ekklesia* was the use of the word in the Greek translation of the Old Testament. There *ekklesia* stands usually for the Hebrew term—itself secular—*kahal* = the assembly called together. What is decisive is the explicitly or implicitly added qualification "of the Lord" or "of Yahweh." The ecclesia of God is more than the occasional event of gathering. The ecclesia is the assembly of the group previously chosen by God, which gathers around God as its center. The term is used in a religious and cultic sense and increasingly understood in an eschatological sense: ecclesia as the true eschatological congregation of God. When the primitive community adopted the designation of ecclesia, it was deliberately asserting a larger claim: to be the true assembly of God, the true congregation of God, the true eschatological people of God which comes together in the name and spirit of Jesus Christ—that is, the ecclesia of Jesus Chris."[56]

---

[55] The Church in *New Advent Catholic Encyclopedia*, http://www. newadvent.org/cathen/03744a.htm (accessed May 12, 2008).

[56] Hans Küng, *On Being a Christian.* (New York: Image Books, 1984), 479.

It is clear from the above quotations that the seeds for the Church's existence were already well in place before the Church's physical foundation. In the Old Testament, God had already chosen a people for himself, through whom he will establish the new and universal covenant that will bring into one fold not just one race, but people from all nations, races, and languages. This community became established in the New Testament as the Church. Affirming this concept of the Church, Vatican II stated, "The Church is God's farm or field. In this field, the ancient olive tree grows whose holy roots were the patriarchs and in which the reconciliation of Jews and Gentiles has been achieved and will continue to be achieved. The church has been planted by the heavenly farmer as a choice vineyard."[57]

The physical manifestation of the Church began with the incarnation. By taking flesh, Christ gathered a new community of believers to himself. It is this community, not yet a church, that later became known as the Church, that is a gathering of those who follow the teachings of Christ. Defining the Church in connection with Christ, Hans Küng said:

> The Church might be briefly defined as the community of those who believe in Christ. More precisely: not founded by Jesus, but emerging after his death in his name as crucified and yet living, the community of those who have become involved in the cause of Jesus Christ and who witness to it as hope for all men. Before Easter, there was nothing more than an eschatological collective movement. A congregation, a Church, came into existence only after Easter and this too was eschatologically oriented: at first its basis was not a cult of its own, a constitution of its own, an organization of its own with definite ministries, but simply and solely the profession of faith in this Jesus as the Christ.[58]

---

57   *Lumen Gentium*, 6.

58   Küng, *On Being a Christian*, 478.

Küng in this passage is not denying that Christ is the founder of Church, as has been maintained in the official teachings of the Church. Rather he is saying that explicitly Christ did not found the Church as an organized institution with its rites and ministries. It is good to note that Christ lived and died as a Jew, never as a Christian. Nevertheless, Küng affirmed strongly that implicitly Christ is the founder of the Church, that is, what emerged as a Church was dependent upon his life, actions and teachings. It was an appreciation and application of this life and teachings of Christ by his followers that gave birth to the Church. Accordingly, Küng, in another work, *The Church*, wrote:

> The origins of the Church do not lie solely in the intention and message of Jesus in the pre-Easter period, but in the whole history of *Jesus' life and ministry*: that is, in the entire action of God in Jesus Christ, from Jesus' birth, his ministry and the calling of the disciples, through to his death and resurrection and the sending of the Spirit to witness to his resurrection. Not the words and instructions of Jesus in the time before Easter alone, but the action of God in resurrecting the crucified Christ and in pouring out the Spirit, turned the group of those who believed communally in the risen Jesus into a community of those who, in contrast to the unbelieving ancient people of God, could claim to be the new eschatological people of God.[59]

The theology of Vatican II is clearly expressed in Küng's expression of the Church as the people of God. The Church is therefore the people whom Christ called together through the institution of the new covenant in his blood; a people made up of not Jews only but also Gentiles. A people brought together as one body under the headship of Christ. A people who are reborn not

---

[59]   Hans Küng, *The Church*. (New York: Sheed and Ward, 1967), 76.

according to the desire of the flesh but by the will of the Spirit. A people made new by the washing of the word, by water and by the Spirit (cf. I Cor. 11: 25; Col 1: 18; Jon 3:5; 1 Pet 2:9-10).[60] Put briefly, "The Church is the Body of Christ and the Creation of the Holy Spirit, as well as the pilgrim People of God. It is a community constituted by Baptism and the Lord's Supper, and it exists at both local and universal levels."[61]

To this Body of Christ and the People of God belongs a membership transcending cultures and boundaries. It is a membership open to all beginning with the baptized but not limited to them. Expressing this understanding, the Code of Canon Law stated "Christ's faithful are those who, since they are incorporated into Christ through baptism, are constituted the people of God."[62] Continuing, Vatican II proclaimed:

> Finally, those who have not yet received the Gospel are related in various ways to the people of God. In the first place, we must recall the people to whom the testament and the promises were given and from whom Christ was born according to the flesh. On account of their fathers this people remains most dear to God, for God does not repent of the gifts He makes nor the calls He issues. Nevertheless, the plan of salvation also includes those who acknowledge the Creator. In the first place, amongst these there are the Moslems, who, professing to hold the faith of Abraham, along with us adore the one and merciful God, who on the last day will judge mankind. Nor is God far distant from those who in shadows and images seek the unknown God, for it is He who gives to all men life and breath and all things, and as Savior wills that all men be saved. Those also can

---

60   *Lumen Gentium*, nos. 7, 9.

61   McBrien, *Catholicism*, 695-696.

62   Canon 204.

attain to salvation who through no fault of their own
do not know the Gospel of Christ or His Church, yet
sincerely seek God and moved by grace strive by their
deeds to do His will as it is known to them through the
dictates of conscience.[63]

The Church, in the understanding of Vatican II is therefore
all-embracing. In addition, this is truly according to the mind of
Christ. Like in Niebuhr's view of Christ, the Church, as universal
agent of salvation, relates to culture in fives ways, namely, the
Church is against culture. She is against cultures because she
challenges cultures with the true message of Christ as means of
purifying the culture of what is contrary to divine will, and human
dignity. The Church is of culture. She is of culture because the
universal Church exists in a particular, local church. She meets
people in their culture and takes flesh among people of various
cultures. The local Church accordingly is defined as a church
incarnated in a people, a church indigenous and inculturated.[64]
Again, though the Church is of a culture, it is at the same time
above culture. The Church while taking root in all the cultures
of the world is herself not identical with any particular culture.
This is primarily because while all cultures are natural in origin
the Church is divine. Hence:

> The church, as has been seen, is a society formed of
> living men, not a mere mystical union of souls. As
> such, it resembles other societies. Like them, it has its
> code of rules, its executive officers, and its ceremonial
> observances. Yet it differs from them more than it
> resembles them: for it is a supernatural society. The
> Kingdom of God is supernatural alike in its origin, in

---

[63] *Lumen Gentium*, no. 16

[64] Oliver A. Onwubiko, *Theory and Practice of Inculturation: An African Perspective.* (Enugu: Snaap Press, 1992), 2.

> the purpose at which it aims, and in the means at its
> disposal. Other kingdoms are natural in their origin;
> and their scope is limited to the temporal welfare of
> their citizens.[65]

Furthermore, Church and culture are in paradox. This paradoxical relationship is seen mainly in the conflict that occur between the Church and culture in the attempt to incarnate herself within that culture. This is in accordance with the human nature that resists whatever it thinks to be alien and offensive to its culture. This paradoxical relationship is witnessed especially in the area of persecution that the Church has suffered through the ages, and in the persecution that various cultures have suffered in the hands of the Church at various times. Finally, the Church is the transformer of culture. The transforming effect of the Church on culture is seen in the positive impacts that the Church has made and is seen in the long-term affect the Church has had on any community it has entered.

All these relationships expressed above take place in the process of incarnating the Christian message in any culture by the Church. The Igbo land is no exception, as we shall see later.

2.3 INCULTURATION IN THE MISSION OF THE CHURCH.

This section deals with the Church's teaching and practice of inculturation from the early Church prior to the Second Vatican Council. This survey is not meant to be exhaustive because of the scope of this work. We shall only focus on salient points, teachings and actions on inculturation. However, it must be pointed out that as we survey the positive statements and attitudes of the Church towards culture, it is important to remember that the Church has also, at times, portrayed native cultures as evil and barbaric, and undertaken missionary activities not in terms of

---

[65] The Church in *New Advent Catholic Encyclopedia*, http://www. newadvent.org/cathen/03744a.htm (accessed May 12, 2008).

inculturation but in the form of western imperialism. Native cultures were seen as mundane while the Church is pure and holy. Commenting on this attitude, McBrien said:

> Although it cannot simply be conceded that this was the original attitude (the Church against people's culture) of the Christian community towards the world, it surely was an answer which appeared very early in the history of the Church. The First Letter of John counsels the faithful against loving the world, for the world is under the power of evil. It is a dying world destined to pass to away . . . The same negative orientation is found in the writings of Tertullian (*Apology and On Idolatry*), and later was significantly present in the monastic movement of the Catholic Church . . . [66]

We shall discuss more on this in 2.4. For now, our attention is on the positive attitude of the Church towards culture in her missionary activities.

In the Christian tradition, the practice of inculturation has been known since the foundation of the Church. As we have already noted, the incarnation is the theological basis of inculturation. The Lord and founder of the Church was born, lived and communicated his message within the culture of his time. As a historical religion, and following the example of the Master, inculturation is part of the Church's history. A by-product of this historical process is a certain accumulation of cultural elements, beginning with the cultures of the Bible and going through a long period of successive inculturations. To start with,

> It [Christianity] came to birth in the highly developed culture of Palestine, at a point where the Jewish, Greek, and Roman cultures intersected. It drew its

---

[66] McBrien, *Catholicism*, 407.

vocabulary, images, rituals, and organization in great part from Judaism of the day. It then matured as a religion by interacting with other cultures of the ancient world—notably those of Greece and Rome.[67]

The Church through the centuries in her evangelizing mission has never lost sight of the inseparable connection between humans and culture, and between the message of Christ and culture. She realizes that Christianity has never existed and could not conceivably exist without culture. Human cultures have always provided Christianity with the languages and visible forms by which it expresses and communicates itself. As expressed by Pope John Paul II:

> It is forever true that the path of culture is the path of man, and it is on this path that man encounters the One who embodies the values of all cultures and fully reveals the man of each culture to himself. The Gospel of Christ the incarnate Word finds its home along the path of culture and from this path; it continues to offer its message of salvation and eternal life.[68]

Already in the First century, Justin (d. 165) had made a case for the need of inculturation in the mission of the early Church. He argued that the Eternal Logos is at the heart of culture.[69] Justin was an expert in discovering Christian "types" in the works of pagan authors. He produced a veritable catalogue of pagan types for the cross of Christ,

---

[67] Thomas P. Rausch, *Evangelizing America*. (New Jersey: Paulist Press, 2004), 14.

[68] John Paul II, "Message to the Bishops of Nigeria at Lagos", on February 15, 1982, in *The Popes Speaks on African Traditional Religion and Cultural Values*. http://www.afrikaworld.net/afrel/atr-popes.htm (accessed May 14, 2008).

[69] Henry Bettenson, ed., *The Early Christian Fathers.* (New York: Oxford University Press, 1956), 60.

chief among them being the mast to which Odysseus was bound as he sailed past the sirens. St Clement of Alexandria developed this image and later Christian commentators on the Iliad and the odyssey continued to hail Jesus as the Christian Odysseus. Socrates was compared sometimes to Moses and sometimes to Christ himself, put to death by the enemies of reason and the Logos.[70] Drawing from the Old and New Testaments, St. Irenaeus (AD 130), cited by Bettenson, made a very insightful point in support of inculturation in the mission of the early Church:

> The marriage of Moses to an Ethiopian woman whom he made a woman of Israel prefigured the grafting of the wild olive on the true olive to share in its fruitfulness. For he who was born in the flesh as the Messiah was sought for by his own people to be slain, but escaped death in Egypt, that is among the gentiles, and sanctified the infants there, and hence brought into being a Church in that land . . . The marriage of Moses was a type of a mystical marriage of Jesus, and the Ethiopian bride signifies the Church of the Gentiles.[71]

It would seem that there was at least some interaction between the worlds of the Old and New Testament and African culture. As observed by Pope Paul VI, "The Church of the West did not hesitate to make use of the resources of African writers, such as Tertullian, Optatus of Milevis, Origen, Cyprian, and Augustine."[72]

---

[70] Jaroslav Pelikan, *Jesus Through the Centuries: His Place in the History of Culture*. (New Haven: Yale University Press, 1999), 41-45.

[71] Bettenson, ed., *The Early Christian Fathers*, 93.

[72] Paul VI, Address at the Symposium of African Bishops in Kampala on July 31, 1969, in "The Popes Speaks on African Traditional Religion and Cultural Values". http://www.afrikaworld.net/afrel/atr-popes.htm (accessed May 14, 2008).

Nevertheless, this is more of a 'consolation prize' for today's African Church. Although these individuals were North African, North Africa was part of the Roman Empire, making them members of the same Greco-Roman culture that shaped early Christianity.

The relation between the Church and the Gentile culture became an issue when Christianity became an official religion of the Roman Empire, and Constantine I (306-337 A.D.), the Roman Emperor, himself became a Christian. To fit in within the society and to make her mission relevant, she had to inculturate herself and her message with the culture of the Empire, by adopting the imperial Roman culture. Accordingly:

> She (the Church) embraced the imperial culture, absorbing its symbols of authority, language, institutions, legal systems and military terminologies. But there was a replacement of idolatrous festivals with Christian celebrations. The birth of Christ, Christmas, was celebrated in place of the birth of the "sun-god" in Mithriac religion. It must be noted that a type of similarity—the feast of the 'true sun of Justice", the *"morning star which never sets"* replaced the sun-god.[73]

This marriage between the Church and the culture of the imperial Roman Empire left a lasting mark in the structure and organization of the Church, sometimes making it difficult to adapt to structures of other cultures.

The Church through the ages, though not always, in her mission of evangelization, has made efforts to respects the religions and cultures of peoples and wishes in her contact with them to preserve all that is noble, true and good in their religion and cultures. A clear example is seen already in a 7th century letter sent by Pope Gregory the Great (590-604) to Abbot Mellitus, a missionary, on his departure to join St. Augustine in Britain in

---

[73]   Onwubiko, *Theory and Practice of Inculturation*, 75.

AD 601. Part of the letter is cited by Shorter in his book *Towards a Theology of Inculturation*:

> Bishop Augustine, we wish to inform you that we have been giving careful thought to the affairs of the English, and have come to the conclusion that the temples of the idols in that country should on no account be destroyed. He is to destroy the idols, but the temples themselves are to be aspersed with holy water, alters set up, and relics enclosed in them. For if these temples are well built, they are to be purified from devil-worship, and dedicated to the service of the true God. In this way, we hope that the people, seeing that its temple are not destroyed, may abandon idolatry and resort to these places as before, and may come to know and adore the true God.[74]

In contrast to Gregory's more limited perspective, who, by referring to the religion of the native as "devil-worship", lacked the essential respect for other people's culture and religion that is required for effective inculturation, in 1659 the Sacred Congregation for the Propagation of the Faith, the Office in charge of mission and missionary activities in the Catholic Church, gave the following instructions to Apostolic Vicars of foreign missions:

> Do not in any way attempt, and do not on any pretext persuade these people to change the rites, habits and customs, unless they are openly opposed to religion and good morals. For what could be more absurd than to bring France, Spain, Italy or any other European country to China[75]

---

74 Shorter, *Towards a Theology of Inculturation*, 141-142.

75 J. Neuner & Jacque Dupuis, eds., *The Christian Faith: In the Doctrinal Documents of the Catholic Church*. (London: Image Books, 1986), 309.

Efforts were made to keep to these instructions by the missionaries, though their activities in most places proved otherwise, as we shall see in the later part of this work.

Following the footstep of his predecessors on the missionary activities of the Church in relation to culture, Pope Pius XII, in 1951 said:

> The Church from the beginning down to our own time has always followed this wise practice: let not the gospel, on being introduced into any new land, destroy or extinguish whatever its people possess that is naturally good, just or beautiful. For the Church, when she calls people to a higher culture and a better way of life under the inspiration of the Christian religion, does not act like one who recklessly cuts down and uproots a thriving forest. No, she grafts a good scion upon the wild stock that it may bear a crop of more delicious fruit.[76]

The history of the development of the Catholic liturgy is full of how rites, gestures, words, etc., were taken over from pagan cultures and worship and utilized for Christian teaching and worship. According to Robertson

> The Christian liturgy grew by absorbing details from pagan cults. The birth story is similar to many nativity myths in the pagan world. The Christ had to have a Virgin for a mother. Like the image of the child-god in the cult of Dionysus, he was pictured in swaddling clothes in a basket manger. He was born in a stable like Horus—the stable temple of the Virgin Goddess, Isis, Queen of heaven. Again, like Dionysus, he turned water into wine; like Aesculapius, he raised men from the dead and gave sight to the blind; and like Attis and

---

[76]   Shorter, *Towards a Theology of Inculturation*, 184

Adonis, he is mourned and rejoiced over by women. His resurrection took place, like that of Mithras, from a rock tomb.[77]

Having so far seen ample evidences of the Church's openness in relation to culture, and the practice of inculturation in the mission of the Church, let us now turn our attention to the other side of story, since the attitude of the Church to the people in mission lands and their culture was not always positive

2.4 WESTERN IMPERIALISM OR EVANGELIZATION?

The nineteenth century saw a renewed zeal in the missionary activities of the Church in evangelizing the nations and cultures of the world. As expressed by Bokenkotter, "The spiritual revival of the Catholic Church during the nineteenth century found an important outlet in missionary zeal, and a whole new period of mission began. Historians generally give Pope Gregory XVI (1831-46) credit for inaugurating this new epoch."[78]

The nineteenth century in Europe also witnessed the scrambling and partitioning of Africa and Asia among the European Nations. This was a period of colonialism and the age of imperialism.[79] The missionaries and the colonial masters moved hand in the hand to their respective territories. The mission of the Church was fashioned in line with the imperial structure of territorial jurisdictions. On this, Udeani noted that:

---

[77] J. M. Robertson, *Pagan Christs*. (New York: Barns & Nobles, 1996), 68.

[78] Thomas Bokenkotter, *A Concise History of the Catholic Church*. (New York: Image Books, 1990), 320.

[79] Cecil Rhodes, "Cape to Cairo" in *The Age of Imperialism*. http:// www.fresno.K12.ca.us/schools/s090/lloyd/imperialism.htm (accessed July 18, 2008)

It is important to establish how the Church understood herself, namely the ecclesiology of the respective periods of the missionary activities . . . [The] ecclesiology behind the missionary activities was not much inspired by salvation history, but was bound with a juridical apologetic understanding of the Church. This territorial conception explains why the mission and missionary activities were understood in the sense of territory in which the mass of people were yet to be brought to the Christian faith. Conceived in an ecclesiocentric manner, conversion was understood as a radical break with one's history in every area of life . . ."[80]

This approach to mission was influenced by Western imperialism and colonization, whose goal was not to evangelize but to 'Christianize' and Westernize all races and cultures.

Moving into Asia, the missionaries continued the western bias and imperialism that saw the Asians and their culture as inferior, and as people who needed the civilizing influence of Western Christianity. It is on record that after 1922, the Chinese and other Asian nations developed a strong anti-Christian movement in protest not to Christianity as a religion, but to a westernized and imperial form of Christianity[81]. As reported by Bokenkotter:

Christianity was denounced as a tool of imperialism . . . Coming to China in the spring of 1902, Pere Lebbe was shocked by the attitude of the missionaries. European and Chinese priests ate at separate tables . . . The Chinese seminaries were given inferior courses to keep them humble. The faithful had to kneel when greeting a missionary and were not permitted to sit in his presence.

---

[80] Chibueze Udeani, *Inculturation as Dialogue: Igbo Culture and the Message of Christ*, (Amsterdam: Rodopi, 2007), 74-5.

[81] Bokenkotter, *A Concise History of the Catholic Church*, 322.

Prospective converts were enticed to instructions by gifts of food or money.[82]

Coming to Africa, the situation was no less different. It was missionary activity mixed with colonialism and imperialism. Commenting on this, Benjamin Ray said that it was:

> Only when European colonialism became firmly rooted in the sub-Saharan Africa in the late nineteen century did Christian missionaries and their African catechist succeed in making large number of converts. Under colonialism, the missionaries were partners with the Western political and economic forces that introduced a wide range of Western values and institution . . . while also indoctrinating Africans with a sense of racial inferiority and a strong dislike for their own religion and culture. Under these circumstances, conversion to Christianity amounted to "conversion" to a whole new culture: colonialism.[83]

Although the late nineteenth and early twentieth century popes tried to present guideline on the missionary activities of the Church, a good number of them were still tied to the concept of exporting western Christianity to mission lands with its imperial baggage and biases. According to Udeani:

> The succession of popes had different views of the mission, which are reflected in their respective encyclicals. These encyclicals, for example Sancta Dei Civita (1880, Leo XIII), Maximum Illud (1919, Benedict XV), Rerum Ecclesiae (1926, Pius XI), Fidei Donum (1957,

---

[82] Ibid.

[83] Benjamin C. Ray, *African Religions: Symbol, Ritual and Community,* 2*nd ed.* (New Jersey: Prentice Hall, 2000), 170.

Pius XII), Princepis Pastorum (1959), especially as the mission left the European cultural world and entered other cultures, were conceived principally as answers and guideline for practical missionary activities and the problems being encountered. Some important aspects were not considered in these documents, including the social situation of the areas where the missionary activity was taking place and the political transformation taking place through colonialism.[84]

The above situation reflected the missionary theology of the First Vatican Council (1869-1870). This council, with it's Thomistic theological definitions, was hostile to "Modernism, as well as towards history and cultural pluralism. Anti-Modernism became the bulwark of classist theology, as well as the last and most formidable obstacle to inculturation."[85] Vatican I and its anti-Modernist aftermath found juridical expression in the 1917 Code of Canon Law. The Code imposed a practical uniformity on the universal Church. This precluded the possibility of a multicultural Church. Again, the reinforcement of theological intellectualism by *Vatican I's* anti-Modernism rendered popular culture irrelevant.[86]

The above-described situation was not favorable for the universal mission of the Church. The Second Vatican Council took cognizance of this and in its document on missions, *Ad Gentes,* called for the rooting out of all vestiges of Christian cultural imperialism. Let us now turn our attention to the Second Vatican Council; the council that truly shaped and reshaped the teaching, theology and mission of the Church as we know it today.

---

[84]   Chibueze Udeani, *Inculturation as Dialogue,* 79.

[85]   Shorter, *Towards a Theology of Inculturation,* 116.

[86]   Ibid, 167.

2.5 VATICAN II AND THE THEOLOGY OF INCULTURATION.

Of all the 21 Ecumenical Councils of the Church, the Second Vatican Council (1962-1965) can rightly be said to be the council most open to people and their culture. With this council emerged a growing sensitivity towards the cultural traditions of peoples who are evangelized. Although the word *inculturation* did not appear in the 16 documents produced by the Council, the council itself was an inculturated council. For the first time ever,

> Many of the bishops came from Africa, Asia, and Latin America. The universality and catholicity of the Roman Church became visible with the presence and representation of so many different cultures and traditions. The council itself was an exercise in inculturation as the Church tried to open its window to the modern world, with its joys and sorrows, hopes and anxieties.[87]

Although many of the Council's documents have elements of inculturation, the most outstanding documents that spelt out the theology of Vatican II on inculturation are the Constitution on the Sacred Liturgy *Sacrosantum Concilium* promulgated on December 4, 1963, the Dogmatic Constitution on the Church *Lumen Gentium*, November 21, 1964, Decree on the Church's Missionary Activity *Ad Gentes Divinitus,* December 7, 1965, and the Pastoral Constitution on the Church in the Modern World *Gaudium et Spes*, December 7, 1965.

The life of the Church in any community depends on rites, rituals and liturgical celebrations. These rites and rituals make present and celebrate the faith and belief of the community. In them, teachings and doctrines are translated into life and action in what is called liturgy. The Constitution on the Sacred Liturgy, therefore, called for the revision of the liturgy to reflect particular situations and cultures. For the first time permission was given

---

[87]   Schineller, *A Handbook on Inculturation*, 39-40.

to make a shift, where necessary, from Latin to vernacular. The document stated, "But since the use of the vernacular, whether in the Mass, the administration of the sacraments, or in other parts of the liturgy, may frequently be of great advantage to the people, wider use may be made of it, especially in readings, directives and in some prayers and chants."[88]

To show its commitment to inculturation, the Council realized that, it is not the Church alone that gives to other cultures, she in turn also takes from these cultures things that are good and noble and integrate them into her liturgy. The Council here affirmed that:

> Anything in people's way of life which is not indissolubly bound up with superstition and error the Church studies with sympathy, and, if possible, preserves intact. It sometimes even admits such things into the liturgy itself, provided they harmonize with its true and authentic sprit . . . In mission countries, in addition to what is found in the Christian tradition, those elements of initiation may be admitted which are already in use among every people, insofar as they can be adapted to the Christian ritual . . . [89]

With the application of these directives, the liturgy of the Church became more vibrant and appealing to people of various cultures. They can now pray, sing and dance in their own way, use their native language to celebrate and read the scriptures, thereby becoming more at home in the Church.

The tone that was set in this first document was continued in *Lumen Gentium*, the Dogmatic Constitution on the Church. In this document, the Council stated, "The Church fosters and takes to herself, insofar as they are good, the ability, resources, and customs of each people. Taking them to herself, she purifies, strengthens, and

---

[88]   *Sacrosantum Concilium*, n. 35.

[89]   Ibid, nn. 37, 65.

ennobles them."[90] As this quotation indicates, the Church shows a threefold relationship to culture. It selects what is true and good; it purifies what she selects, separating it from things that is unworthy of the gospel; then she elevates even the finest fruits of human endeavor found in that culture by turning them into instruments for the transmission of the truth and grace that comes from God. In line with this theology, the Council affirmed that:

> Whatever good or truth is found amongst them (people and cultures) is looked upon by the Church as a preparation for the Gospel . . . Through her work, whatever good is in the minds and hearts of men, whatever good lies latent in the religious practices and cultures of diverse peoples, is not only saved from destruction but is also cleansed, raised up and perfected unto the glory of God, the confusion of the devil and the happiness of man.[91]

Another document of vital importance in Vatican II's theology of inculturation is the Decree on the Church's Missionary Activity *Ad Gentes Divinitus*. This document can be considered as the blue print of the Church's attitude toward the culture of those she sets out to evangelize. As Aylward Shorter puts it,

> It is difficult to exaggerate the importance of *Ad Gentes* for the development of modern mission theology . . . From the outset stress is laid on human communities and their socio-cultural traditions as the focus of missionary interest. In this context, the analogy of the Incarnation is used for the first time (in the Council's documents).[92]

---

[90] *Lumen Gentium*, n. 13
[91] Ibid, nn. 16, 17.
[92] Shorter, *Towards a Theology of Inculturation*, 195

Bearing in mind the importance of inculturation in the evangelizing mission of the Church, the Council stated:

> For the Gospel message has not yet, or hardly yet, been heard by two billion human beings—and their number is increasing daily—who are formed into large and distinct groups by permanent cultural ties, by ancient religious traditions, and by firm bonds of social necessity . . . The Church, in order to be able to offer all of them the mystery of salvation and the life brought by God, must implant herself into these groups for the same motive which led Christ to bind Himself, in virtue of His Incarnation, to certain social and cultural conditions of those human beings among whom He dwelt.[93]

In order to implant herself into these groups, the universal Church must become a local or particular Church, with all the peculiarities of the people. In order to make herself local, she must take flesh within the culture of the people. That is why the council stated that:

> In harmony with the economy of the Incarnation, the young churches, rooted in Christ and built up on the foundation of the Apostles, take to themselves in a wonderful exchange all the riches of the nations which were given to Christ as an inheritance (cf. Ps. 2:8). They borrow from the customs and traditions of their people, from their wisdom and their learning, from their arts and disciplines, all those things which can contribute to the glory of their Creator, or enhance the grace of their Savior, or dispose Christian life the way it should be.[94]

---

[93]   *Ad Gentes*, n. 10
[94]   Ibid, n. 22.

One of the new dimensions that this document added to the theology of inculturation is the emphasis that for the Church to be universal and at same time local, for her to meet with the actual needs and challenges of inculturation, she must have ministers, who are already at home in the cultures and who will in turn integrate the Christian message into the cultures, without imposing a culture that is foreign. Accordingly, the Council stated:

> The work of implanting the Church in a particular human community reaches a definite point when the assembly of the faithful, already rooted in the social life of the people and to some extent conformed to its culture, enjoys a certain stability and permanence; when it has its own priests, although insufficient, its own religious and laity and possesses those ministries and institutions which are required for leading and spreading the life of the people of God under the leadership of their own bishop.[95]

Another document is the Constitution on the Church in the Modern World *Gaudium et Spes*. The whole of the second chapter of Part Two of this document is devoted exclusively to the study of culture. The key passage of this document is number 58, which discusses the relationship between the Gospel and culture. This number opened by affirming that:

> There are many ties between the message of salvation and human culture. For God, revealing Himself to His people to the extent of a full manifestation of Himself in His Incarnate Son, has spoken according to the culture proper to each epoch. Likewise the Church, living in various circumstances in the course of time, has used the discoveries of different cultures so that in her preaching she might spread and explain the message of Christ to

---

95 Ibid, n.19.

all nations, that she might examine it and more deeply understand it, that she might give it better expression in liturgical celebration and in the varied life of the community of the faithful.[96]

Apart from bringing out the links between the Gospel and culture, the document went further to note that although the Church takes root and spreads the message of Christ within human culture, she is not herself tied exclusively to any one culture. Rather, she enters into communion with different forms of culture, giving to the culture and at the same time taking from the culture. This is exactly what we mean by inculturation. Expressing this view, the Council said:

> The Church, sent to all peoples of every time and place, is not bound exclusively and indissolubly to any race or nation, any particular way of life or any customary way of life, ancient or modern. Faithful to her own tradition and at the same time conscious of her universal mission, she can enter into communion with the various forms of culture, to their enrichment and the enrichment of the Church herself.[97]

When the Church enters in communion with a culture it does not destroy the culture, but it also does not leaves the culture the way it was. When this communion takes place, the Church positively, without malice,

> Combats and removes the errors and evils resulting from the permanent allurement of sin in that culture. She purifies and elevates the morality of peoples. She makes fruitful, as it were from within, the spiritual qualities

---

96   *Gaudium et Spes*, n. 58
97   Ibid.

and traditions of the people. She strengthens, perfects,
and restores them in Christ.[98]

In other words, the intention of the Church is not to destroy the
culture of the people with the negative intention that such a culture
is evil, but through love to exalt the human dignity which otherwise
may have been debased as a result of certain cultural practices. For
example, in Igbo culture, prior to the coming of Christianity, twins
were seen as an abomination and were killed upon birth. Again,
certain cultural rites required human sacrifice. Here, while not
seeing the people as evil, based on their religio-cultural practices, the
Church has educated them on the value, importance and dignity of
the human person, even that of a newborn.

The theology of Vatican II on inculturation outlined in this
chapter forms the basis for incarnating the Christian message in
the Igbo land of Nigeria. This exercise should not be understood
as 'made in Rome', for that would be ecclesial imperialism, not
inculturation. To avoid this, the Igbo bishops should make good
use of the latitude given to them by the Vatican to seek ways of
making the Christian message relevant to the life and condition
of their people. Again, to achieve this result the bishops in
conjunction with their senate of priests should establish in every
parish, which represents the grassroots, a committee that studies,
produces and implements guidelines on inculturation. These
guidelines will necessary differ from parish to parish, depending
on the particular culture of that local parish community. What is
produced and implemented will not be a product of other people's
thinking. In this way, the fruit of inculturation will be a product
of dialogue and interaction between the Church and those living
in the concrete situation of a particular culture, thereby avoiding
western and or ecclesial imperialism.

---

[98] Ibid.

Chapter Three

THE IGBO LAND AND THE CHRISTIAN MESSAGE

3.1 THE IGBO LAND'S RELIGIOUS HERITAGE.

Traditional Igbo society can be described as a homogeneous society; a society where religion enfolds the whole of life. Culture is understood from the religious perspective. As Ejizu puts it, "Religion is the womb of culture in the traditional Igbo background. It permeates most aspects of life, and infuses them with meaning and significance."[99] Social life is regulated by the dictates and principles of religion, and there is no dividing line between the religion, ethics and morality. As a matter of fact, "the gods serve as policemen"[100] in matters relating to the ordering of society and people's life. Accordingly, "Among the Igbo, religion and law are so closely interwoven that many of the powerful legal

---

[99] Christopher Ejizu, *The Influence of African Indigenous Religions on Roman Catholicism, The Igbo Example.* http://www.afrikaworld. net/afrel/ejizu-atrcath.htm (accessed May 18, 2008).

[100] Christopher Ejizu, *Ofo, Igbo Ritual Symbol._*(Enugu: Fourth Dimension Publishers, Ltd, 1986), 90.

sanctions are derived directly from the gods."[101] At this time in Igbo land, a completely secular world did not exist. Everybody is religious and everything is done religiously. The inseparability of religion and the totality of the Igbo people's whole of existence are summarized by a down to earth observation of Major A. G. Leonard, a pioneer British colonial master to Igbo land. In his words, "They (the Igbos) are in the strict and natural sense of the word, a truly and deeply religious people, of whom it can be said, as it has been said of the Hindus, that they eat religiously, drink religiously, bathe religiously, dress religiously, and sin religiously. In few words, the religion of these natives, as I have endeavored to point out is their existence, and their existence is their religion."[102]

Before the advent of the Christianity, the Igbos had already developed a clear concept of a creator God, whom they call *Chineke* (the God who creates), *Chukwu* or *Chi-Ukwu* (the biggest God or Supreme God), *Obasi di n'elu* (the God who lives on high or in heaven). According to E. M. P. Ede, "The issue of God's existence among the Igbos is so obvious that there is not much concern among them about proving formally his existence. Preference is given to views asserting the obviousness of God's existence . . ."[103] The affirmation of the existence and belief in God is expressed in the giving of names like *Chukwudi* (God is), *Chiebuka*, (God is so great).

Although the Igbos believe in the existence and power of the Supreme Being, they, like other African tribes, believe in other deities, who are in relationship with, and often play intermediary roles to the Supreme Being. As expressed by Ikenga Metuh, "The Igbos recognizes some relationship between Chukwu and the Deities . . . The Deities are sometimes referred to as the sons of Chukwu, or his messengers, and sometimes as his manifestations. Sacrifices visibly

---

[101]   Arthur G. Leonard, *The Lower Niger and its Tribes*. (London: Frank Cass, 1906), 30

[102]   Ibid, 429.

[103]   E. M. P. Edeh, *Towards an Igbo Metaphysics*. (Chicago: Loyola Univ. Press, 1985), 118.

offered to the Deities are said by the Igbo to be ultimately received by Chineke, the former being only mediators."[104]

Associated to the worship of God and the deities is the worship and/or veneration of the ancestors. The ancestors are held in a very high esteem in Igbo culture and religion. They are far closer to the people than the gods are. The ancestors are believed to be the guardians of family affairs, customs and traditions and ethical norms. Offence in these matters is ultimately an offence against the ancestors who in that capacity, like the gods, act as invisible police of the families and communities.[105] The symbol of the ancestral spirit and authority is the *OFO*.[106] Although physically dead, the ancestors are said to be spiritually alive. According to Mbiti:

> The ancestors are the living-dead. They are the closest links that men have with the spirit world . . . [They] are bilingual: they speak the language of men, with whom they lived until 'recently'; and they speak languages of the spirits and of God, to whom they are drawing nearer ontologically. These are the 'spirits' with which African peoples are most concerned: it is through the living-dead that the spirit world becomes personal to men. They are still part of the human families, and people have personal memories of them.[107]

---

[104] E. I. Metuh, *African Religions in Western Conceptual Schemes: The Problem of Interpretation.* (Onitsha: Imico, 1991), 40.

[105] E. I. Metuh, *Comparative Studies of African Traditional Religion.* (Onitsha: Imico, 1987), 149.

[106] The *Ofo* is a carved wooden staff made from a special tree called *Abosi*. It is a central symbol of Igbo spirituality. It is a symbol of authority entrusted to the head of the lineage. It is also a symbol of justice, righteousness, and truth. It also plays many important roles in the cultural, social and political life of the Igbo.

[107] John S. Mbiti, *African Religions and Philosophy,* 2nd ed. (Ibadan: Heinemann Books, 1969), 82.

Another aspect worth mentioning in the religio-socio-cultural life of the Igbo people is the place of ritual ceremonies, accompanied by sacred music and dances. There is ritual for every event and state of life from birth to death. According to E. C. Eze, "Rituals often occur according to the lifecycle of the year. There are hunting rituals as well as those marking the rhythm of agricultural and human life. Every deity has its own ritual, including choice of objects for sacrifice, time of the day, week, month, or year to make required sacrifices."[108] Some of these rituals are also intended for healing and are performed by special medicine men or healers. These medicine men act as medical personnel and doctors. There are rituals for asking favors from the gods and for atonement for wrongdoings.

Every event is also a celebration. The celebration may be joyful or mournful depending on the occasion and circumstance. Most rituals and acts of worship, as well as other ceremonies, do take place in sacred places like shrines, village squares, evil forests, and rivers depending on the nature of the event, celebration and/ or sacrifice required.

In Igbo traditional society, a man is considered wealthy and successful based on the number of wives and children he has as well as the number of titles he has taken. In fact title taking was a very prestigious achievement. Using Okonkwo as an example, Chinua Achebe described in *Things Fall Apart*:

> Among these people, a man was judged according to his worth . . . Okonkwo won fame in the nine villages. He was a wealthy farmer and has just married his third wife. To crown it all he had taken two titles. And although he was still young, he was already one of the greatest men of his time. Age was respected among his people, but

---

[108] E. C. Eze, "Religion and Philosophy" in *Word Era Encyclopedia*, vol. 10, Edited by Pierre-Damien Mvuyekure (New York: Thomas-Gale, 2003), 247.

achievement was revered. As the elders said, if a child washed his hands he could eat with his kings. Okonkwo had clearly washed his hands and so he eats with kings and elders.[109]

What has been said so far is just a summary of the life of the Igbo people. There is quite a lot still to be said about the community life of the people, but such may be too much to accommodate within the scope this work. However, with the coming of the Christian missionaries, some of the above-mentioned ideals, if not all of them, were branded fetish and paganic and had to be evangelized.

3.2 THE MISSION AND MISSIONARY ACTIVITIES OF THE CHURCH IN IGBO LAND.

The missionary activities of the Church in Nigeria began in the late 15th and early 16th centuries through Catholic Portuguese missionaries. This effort was short lived. A vibrant and lasting Christianity eventually came to Nigeria in general and Igbo land in particular in the 1800s. The first missionary activity in Igbo land that bore lasting fruits started in 1857. This time Protestants through the Church Missionary Society (CMS) took the initiative. The Catholic missionaries of the Holy Ghost Congregation led by Fr. Joseph Lutz in 1885 later joined them. Incidentally, both missions began in Onitsha because of its proximity to the river Niger. Tracing the origin of missionary activities in Igbo land, Chibueze Udeani reported that:

> After the initial attempt, which was not able to take off for different reasons, the definite date was 27th July, 1857 when an agreement was finally executed between a missionary group led by Samuel Crowther and Obi Akazua of Onitsha and his councilors to establish a Christian

---

[109] Chinua Achebe, *Things Fall Apart*. (New York: Anchor Books, 1959), 8.

mission station at Onitsha, an Ibo (sic) town on the eastern bank of the river Niger . . . The second missionary effort towards the evangelization of Igboland came from the Roman Catholic missionaries. The first group started in 1885 under the leadership of Joseph Lutz—a French priest . . . His group like those of the CMS was well received by the King and Chiefs of Onitsha. Though the Roman Catholic missionaries started later than the CMS group, they succeeded in penetrating into the interior parts of Igboland and establishing strong footholds . . . A third missionary effort undertaken began with the early Methodist society in 1892, altogether there were some six European-based missionary groups involved in the evangelization of Igboland.[110]

A number of questions that might be raised at this point are, what type of Christianity did the missionaries bring to Igbo land? How did they see the people they came to evangelize? What was their method of evangelism? In addition, what was the initial reaction of the Igbo people to the mission of the Church?

Scholars and historians of the Church's missionary activities in Igbo land are almost in consensus that the Christianity brought to Igbo land by the missionaries, Protestants and Catholics alike, was not the Christianity nurtured and preached by the Apostles, but rather a European-Colonial Christianity that viewed everything from the lenses of European culture. As such, everything that fell short of the European way of life and culture was anti-Christian, fetish and diabolical. Expressing this fact of colonial Christianity in Igbo land, Udeani said:

> Christianity's expansion was supported by the British colonial efforts in Igboland. The primary factors were

---

[110] Chibueze Udeani, *Inculturation as Dialogue: Igbo Culture and the Message of Christ.* (Amsterdam: Rodopi, 2007), 98-99.

trade and political control. The different missionary groups came to the interior following the colonialists . . . The Igbos identified the missionaries with the colonial governance and with the standards and values, which this colonial governance intended to inculcate. The missionaries regarded it as one of their tasks to furnish the government with loyal subjects who would assist in the destruction of idolatry, superstition and slavery . . . The missionaries saw the colonial policy as a material instrument of civilization. This instrument was seen as necessary for it would open up the interior parts of Igboland for their missionary activities. There is much evidence of the close alliance between the Catholic missionaries and the colonial government in Igboland.[111]

Consequently, because of colonial Christianity, mixed with western bias, the missionaries described the religion of the Igbo people as "superstition, idolatry, devil's mischief, magic, fetishism, animism, polytheism, ancestor worship, offspring/product of unenlightenment and blooming imagination."[112] The missionaries failed to accord sufficient importance to Igbo culture and tradition. Christianity was preached in an exclusively Western form and identical with European culture. This caused the alienation of many Igbos from the Christian faith.[113] Commenting on this attitude of the missionaries not just to Igbo land in particular but to Africa in general, Peter Schineller said, "When Christianity went from Europe to Africa, it often traveled with the colonizers. Armed with the myth of the superiority of western European culture, they simply transplanted western Christianity to African soil, showing little respect, and often disdain, for traditional

---

[111] Ibid, 99-102.
[112] Udeani, *Inculturation as Dialogue*, 81-82.
[113] Thomas Bokenkotter, *A Concise History of the Catholic Church.* (New York: Image Books, 1990), 327.

local cultures."[114] Continuing, John Mbiti observed, " . . . in the village and in the town, one aspect of mission Christianity is that it is superficial, blended with Western culture and materialism and still estranged to the depths of African societies."[115]

To evangelize the people and implant their brand of Christianity, the missionaries adopted a negative approach. They began by wiping out what they considered satanic and unbecoming of the Gospel and what was considered barbaric by colonial masters, coming from the same stock and religio-cultural background as the missionaries.

Wherever the missionaries went, native customs, culture, traditions and religion were their first target. They had at their core a subtle mix of encouragement and coercion in Christianizing and civilizing the indigenous peoples and prodding them to see their heritage as dark colors of evil, everything that existed before the advent of western Christianity and 'civilization' was stamped heathen. These they destroyed either forcefully, with the help of the colonial army or through their teachings. Evangelization for them was "a crusade against the devil, the inspirer of heathen religions and institutions."[116] Expressing this in the words of H. Rucker, as quoted by Chibueze Udeani:

> It is no exaggeration to maintain that the principal missionary attitude towards Igbo cultures and religions has been one of negation. All in all, many missionaries acted on the "tabula rasa" principle, demolishing everything that appeared as magic and, according to Western understanding, as an obstacle to Christianity. This they saw as defending the biblical monotheism against idolatry.[117]

---

[114] Peter Schineller, *A Handbook on Inculturation.* (New York: Paulist Press, 1990). 11.

[115] Mbiti, *African Religions and Philosophy*, 232.

[116] Udeani, *Inculturation as Dialogue*, 84-85.

[117] Ibid, 82.

The activities of the missionaries caused many upheavals in the socio-cultural and religious life in Igbo land. The missionaries and their converts desecrated things that were culturally and religiously sacred. Using the case of Nri as an example,

> Converts were encouraged to flout authority of the *ozo* men, burn their ritual objects, break the taboos and reveal the secret of ritual mask . . . the encouragement of the destruction of traditional objects of worship spread out over all Igbo land. In this operation, the educated Christians, who were mostly teachers and pastors, were used. They condemned the traditional title system, marriage, rituals, songs, arts, and labeled them "things of Satan".[118]

In addition, Igbo native names were also looked upon as devilish. Hence, the new converts at baptism had to drop their names and adopt new names, which had to be English or Jewish, and their mode of dressing was also changed to show that they had accepted Christianity and were now born again.[119]

It is good to note that the missionaries and the mission they brought to Igbo land totally ignored or contradicted the official teachings of the Church, which is respect and tolerance towards the culture and religion of other people especially those in mission land, as we have seen in chapter two of this work. This teaching is re-echoed in our time in the teachings of Vatican II and the magisterium. For example,

> In Lumen Gentium 13, and Ad Gentes 22, the Second Vatican Council in appreciating the customs and ways of life of each people, insists on the need for the missionary effort to assimilate these into the patrimony

---

[118] Jacob K. Olupona, ed., *African Traditional Religions in Contemporary Society*, (New York: Paragon House, 1991), 113

[119] Ibid, 117.

of the Church. In Evangelii Nuntiandi 20, Paul VI makes mandatory the incorporation of human cultures into the building of the kingdom of God as a necessary requisite of Evangelization in today's world. And John Paul II in such documents as Catechesi Tradendae 53, Redemptoris Missio 52-54, and Ecclesia in Africa 42-43, makes dialogue with cultures an essential component of Evangelization and gospel proclamation.[120]

However, to be fair to the missionaries and their mission in Igbo land, it is good to point out that they saw something positive in Igbo land that became a vehicle to spread their message. That is, the Igbo language. According to Christopher Ejizu,

> In spite of their disdain for the indigenous religious culture, pioneer Christian missionaries in general (whether Roman Catholic or Protestant), knew pretty well they had to depend on the indigenous language to communicate the gospel message to the people. While the doctrines and principal religious ideas remained those of their respective Christian traditions, the local language as the primary medium of communication with their host, provided the bulk of the concepts, terms and linguistic symbols and imageries. That is not all. It set limit to thought and understanding of the received message of the missionaries.[121]

---

[120] Paul Bekye, *African Traditional Religion in Church Documents.* http://www.afrikaworld.net/afrel/atraxadocs.htm (accessed May 22, 2008)

[121] Christopher Ejizu, *The Influence of African Indigenous Religions on Roman Catholicism, The Igbo Example.* http://www.afrikaworld. net/afrel/ejizu-atrcath.htm (accessed May 22, 2008)

Another area worth mentioning is that the missionary activities brought to an end the *OSU* caste system that was practiced in some part of Igbo land. (An *OSU* is someone dedicated to the gods as a sacrificial offering). It is also a common knowledge that missionaries abolished the killing of twins of Igbo land.

The missionaries also affected Igbo land positively in the area of education, although the education they brought was a means of winning converts from the traditional religion. Most important was the introduction of western medicine to Igbo land by the missionaries. According to Joseph Awolalu,

> In addition to Western education, medicine and technology also came through the missionaries. These improved people's health, reduced infant mortality, put under control diseases and ailments, which people dreaded—for example, small pox, malaria, stomach pain, and the like—discouraged superstition, fear, and brought about better conditions of living.[122]

In sum, there are both positive and negative effects of the Church's missionary activities in Igbo land. The positive effects are seen more on the social life, while the negative effects are seen in the religio-cultural life of the people. Some Igbos accepted the fruits of Christianity on the social life, but rejected it on the religio-cultural life. Some Igbos, although they are Christians, still feel a vacuum in their worship of God. One thing is clear: the missionaries in Igbo land never thought of their mission in terms of inculturation. They saw the Christian message and Igbo culture and religion as oil and water that can never mix. We shall see the outcome of this missionary approach in the next section of this chapter.

---

[122] Olupona, ed., *African Traditional Religions in Contemporary Society*, 114

3.3 THE CHRISTIAN MESSAGE AND IGBO CULTURE AT A CROSSROAD.

The brand of Christianity brought by the missionaries to Igbo land ended up putting the Igbos at a crossroad of faith. It created a division of loyalty between the gospel message and the native religion and culture. To use the words of Idowu:

> It is now becoming clear to the most optimistic of Christian evangelists that the main problem of the church in Africa today is the divided loyalties of most of her members between Christianity with its Western categories and practices on one hand, and the traditional religion on the other.[123]

A response to this division produced two types of reaction: a compromising reaction and a violent reaction. The compromising reaction saw the Igbos as half-Christian and half followers of native religion and culture. The violent reaction saw not only a battle of words but also physical conflicts between the Christians and adherents of Igbo culture and religion.

At the crossroad of compromise, the words of a Zairean poet vividly express the situation, "Oh unhappy Christian, Mass in the morning, witch doctor in the evening. Amulet (Charm) in the pocket, Bible in the hand and scapular/medals around the neck."[124] The reason for the above situation is not far fetched. The Igbos, like every other African tribe, look to religion for succor in strictly personal matters relating to the passages of life and the crises of life like, sickness, failure in business, death, witchcraft, and childlessness. This succor was not found in the missionary Churches because of their rigidity and orthodoxy.

---

[123]   E. Bolaji Idowu, *African Traditional Religion: A Definition.* (New York: Orbis Books, 1975), 205-6.

[124]   Nathaniel I. Ndiokwere, *The African Church, Today and Tomorrow,* vol. I. (Onitsha: Effective Key Publisher, 1994), 53.

They were not in touch with, or ignorant of, the people's worldview regarding the role of religion in daily life; hence the desire of the Igbo Christians to get from their native religion what missionary religion could not provide. Attesting to this fact from a personal Igbo experience, Cardinal Francis Arinze in a letter from the Pontifical Council for Interreligious Dialogue, Vatican City, addressed to the Presidents of the Episcopal Conferences of Africa and Madagascar, dated March 25, 1988 said:

> Many Christians, at critical moments in their lives, have recourses to practices of the traditional religion, or to 'prayer houses', 'healing homes', 'prophets', witchcraft or fortune-tellers. Some tend to join sects or so-called "Independent Churches" where they feel that certain elements of their culture are more respected.[125]

Expressing this view further, Ndiokwere said:

> Because the European brand of Christianity was neither satisfying to the African, nor did it provide answers or solution to certain African problems . . . there has for long therefore been a painful search for something more satisfying and meaningful to the Africans, especially in the religious sphere . . . He looks for protective charms and amulets and other substances from anywhere."[126]

This anywhere is, of course, outside the Church. A mixture of traditional rituals, sacrifices and prayers with the Christian rites and objects satisfies such longings. Caught up in this situation the Igbo

---

125 Francis Arinze, *Pastoral Attention to African Traditional Religion.* http://www.afrikaworld.net/afrel/vatican.html (accessed May 22, 2008)

126 Ndiokwere, *The African Church, Today and Tomorrow,* vol. I, 36-7.

Christian sees himself in perpetual search of a lost identity. He is neither truly a Christian nor truly a follower of the native religion and culture. He is at a crossroad. As expressed by Bishop Peter Sarpong, "Alas he [the Igbo] searches in vain for his heart's desire in the Catholic Church. The Christian Church in its wake abolishes his cherished institution through which he saw himself."[127] To worsen his situation, a new concept of God, which had no connection with his experience and life was introduced. No proper foundation was laid to inculturate the message of Christ in the hearts and lives of the Igbo people. No bridge was built to connect the past and present of the Igbo people and their culture and religion.[128] Because nature abhors vacuum, the Igbo Christian sees himself comprising the Christian faith with his native religion and culture to make up for what is lacking. Commenting on this, Udeani said:

> Today many Igbo converts maintain a dual relationship. Though converted Christians, they remain consciously and unconsciously deeply rooted in Igbo traditional religion. The fact that irrespective of the conversion into Christianity, the Igbo still flock to their traditional religion should be indicative of the ambiguity existing in their religious life. This shows clearly that there is need for dialogue between Igbo traditional culture and the Message of Christ.[129]

At the crossroad of violence, in which the Igbo people also found themselves because of missionary Christianity, Vincent Mulago has this to say, "Any meeting of two different realities incurs the risk of conflict. We do, in fact, observe at times conflict between the cultural heritage of black Africa and

[127] Schineller, *A Handbook on Inculturation*. 11.
[128] Udeani, *Inculturation as Dialogue*, 88.
[129] Ibid, 214.

Christianity."[130] This was and has been the case especially in places "where Christianity was perceived as allied to colonization, it often generated conflict and was seen by some African leaders and intellectuals as destroying the African way of life."[131] For the Igbos and Africa, in general the attack on culture and religion is an attack on the whole system of people's life that revolves around their religion and culture. This conflict manifest itself in the destruction of traditional cultural and religious artifacts and places of worship by converts who are zealous for their new found faith, and the response by the followers of native religions either by destroying the Christian places of worship or by ostracizing Christians from the community. For a true Igbo, the worst thing that happens to a person is to lose his clan, community and tribal identity. On the other hand, the Christian is threatened with excommunication should he fall back to "pagan" way of life. Articulating this situation, Oliver Onwubiko said,

> Resistance to culture change has been part of the violence in Africa especially on the socio-spiritual level. People have seen their worldview challenged without proper substitution and in some cases; the changes are so fast that some have seen their cultural values collapse and fall apart. Some, in consequence, have instituted themselves into a block of cultural immobility resulting into violent relationship between Christians and non-Christians, on matters of traditional practices based on African Traditional Religion.[132]

---

[130] Olupona, ed., *African Traditional Religions in Contemporary Society*, 128

[131] Richard F. Weir, ed., *The Religious World: Communities of Faith*. (New York: Macmillan Publishers, 1982), 49

[132] Oliver Onwubiko *Echoes From the African Synod*. (Enugu: Snaap Press, 1994), 129.

Here are a few examples of this violence. Recounting an incident that happened between the Christians and traditional religionists in Umuofia village of Igbo land, Chinua Achebe said:

> It was Enoch (a Christian) who touched off the great conflict between the church and clan in Umuofia . . . It happened during the annual ceremony, which was held in honor of the earth deity. At such times, the ancestors of the clan who had been committed to Mother Earth at their death emerged again as *egwugwu* (a masquerader who impersonate one of the ancestral spirits of the village) through tiny ant-holes. One of the greatest crimes a man could commit was to unmask an *egwugwu* in public, or to say or do anything, which might reduce his immortal prestige in the eyes of the uninitiated. And this was what Enoch did . . . [He] tore off his (egwugwu) mask . . . Enoch had killed an ancestral spirit, and Umuofia was thrown into confusion. That night the Mother of the Spirits walked the length and breadth of the clan, weeping her murdered son. It was a terrible night. Not even the oldest man in Umuofia had ever heard such a strange and fearful sound, and it was never to be heard again.[133]

Because of this desecration, the villagers went and destroyed Enoch's house, and Enoch narrowly escaped death. Together with all the egwugwu in the clan, they went to Church. When they left the church, Achebe continued, "The red-earth church was a pile of earth and ashes. And for the moment the spirit of the clan was pacified."[134]

---

[133] Achebe, Things Fall Apart, 186-7.
[134] Ibid, 191.

Another example is a Newspaper report that appeared in one of the Nigerian dailies: *Sunday Tribune*. According to the reporter:

> There was a stampede last Sunday at Ijedodu Village in Isheri-Osun area of Lagos State following the invasion of the Lion of Judah parish of the Eternal Sacred Order of Cherubim and Seraphim Church by a procession of traditional worshippers led by masquerade . . . no sooner than the group of invaders, laced with charms, and dangerous weapons stormed the church auditorium while chanting war songs than tempers rose on both sides. A couple of minutes later, the congregation and the traditionalist were engaged in a free-for-all fight . . . The Otun of Ijedodu, Chief Muniru Ododo, said that the traditional worshippers decided to invade the church because of the desecration of the customs and traditions of the community by the church leadership in the person of Special Apostle Michael A. Balogun and his wife, Senior Prophetess Mojisola Balogun.[135]

The question then is, which way out? The answer is inculturation. However, it must be noted that inculturation is not an easy task, as there are some problems that must be faced, especially within the Igbo context. Identifying these problems and the ways these can be solved or avoided will make room for a fruitful and meaningful inculturation of the Message of Christ in Igbo land.

---

[135] Oladipo Adelowo, "Masquerades, traditional worshippers invade church," *Sunday Tribune*, May 11, 2008. http://www.tribune.com. ng/11052008/news/news15.html (accessed May 23, 2008).

3.4 THE THEOLOGICO-CULTURAL PROBLEMS OF INCULTURATING THE CHRISTIAN MESSAGE IN IGBO LAND.

The concept of inculturation and the practice of it has become commonplace in the Church today. Everyone truly acknowledges that it is indeed a laudable venture and a welcomed development. Nevertheless, in such laudable ventures many problems militate against the realization. At the theologico-cultural level, such problems include authority and dogmatism, resistance to cultural changes, superiority complex and fear of syncretism, theory versus action, and lack of dialogue between the Church and Igbo culture. We shall briefly discuss each of these problems.

i) Authority and dogmatism: The Church hierarchy in Igbo land appears to be more authority conscious and dogmatic than Rome itself in matters of inculturation. The Vatican has given permission to the local ordinaries to adapt the liturgy to suit the local needs of their flock. Even at that, Igbo bishops, in their spirit of authority, still rely heavily on the Vatican for everything regarding inculturation. At times they are so dogmatic that they do not want to 'tamper' with the sacred rituals handed down to them as Apostles through the ages. This is indeed a hindrance to inculturation because unless the hierarchy approves, no proposal on inculturation will be tested nor approved. The role of the hierarchy is indispensible because they regulate, control and moderate the liturgy. The authorities should loosen up a bit so that the work of inculturation will be facilitated. As Ndiokwere advised, "The leaders of the Church in Africa should not pretend to be more Roman than the Pope. Rome or the Pope does not even cherish such inordinate zeal for orthodoxy or faithfulness to the Roman tradition."[136] The time has come for the Igbo bishops, while not neglecting the authority of Rome, to show that they are

---

[136] Nathaniel I. Ndiokwere, *The African Church, Today and Tomorrow,* vol. II. (Enugu: Snaap Press, 1994), 45.

truly the pastors of the flock entrusted to their care and feed them adequately with their native 'meal' by inculturating the liturgy.

ii) Resistance to cultural changes: On the part of the Igbo people, there are those who see inculturation as a destruction of their cultural heritage and the Church's way of neo-colonizing the Igbo people. Because of this understanding, every effort towards inculturating the Christian message into the people's culture is drastically resisted. I have personally witnessed this in some of communities that I have ministered as a priest. Making the same observation, Onwubiko said,

> Resistance to cultural change has been part of the problems in Africa especially on the socio-cultural level . . . Some have instituted themselves into a block of cultural immobility resulting into violent relationship between Christian and non-Christians, on maters of traditional practices based on African traditional religion.[137]

This is indeed a problem for inculturation. To avoid this, the Church must manifest a genuine intention to the people that inculturation is not neo-colonization. This can be done by carrying the people along through dialogue in the process of inculturation. The people should be made to realize that there are positive elements in their culture that the Church can take and make part of her worship. This will remove suspicion and resistance from the Igbo people.

iii) Superiority complex and fear of syncretism: Often times the Church sees herself as having a superior culture in relation to Igbo culture. With this in mind, every thing native is seen as fetish, inferior and unworthy of the Gospel of Christ. Again, the Church has described the Indigenous African Churches as syncretistic because they incorporate native and traditional values in the mode of worship. Consequently, most Church leaders are

---

[137]   Oliver Onwubiko *Echoes From the African Synod.* (Enugu: Snaap Press, 1994), 129

reluctant to engage in the practice of inculturation so as not to water down the Gospel message or empty the Cross of Christ of its power.

The Church must realize that no human race is inferior to the other, and as such, their culture should not be seen as inferior. Respect of a people and their culture is a very important step in the journey of inculturation.

iv) Theory versus action: Over the years, a lot has been said on the need to inculturate the Christian message in Igbo land. Many good sounding theological and cultural principles have been proposed. All these have remained only theoretical. The problem is that of apathy, mostly on the side of local ordinaries and priests that are charged with the grassroots implementations of the proposals. Expressing this problem as it concerns the hierarchy, Shorter rightly observed that:

> The official Church teaches the theology of inculturation with increasing exactness, and even sensitivity, but it does not appear eager to match praxis with theory. Its extreme caution and its policy of gradualness often discourage Christians in the local churches.[138]

Again, some fundamentalists strongly oppose the implementations of those proposals as that will be bringing 'darkness and light together'. Unless theory is matched with action, the idea of inculturation will always remain a mirage.

v) Lack of dialogue between the Church and Igbo culture: This is one of the greatest obstacles to inculturation in Igbo land. The Christian message came into Igbo land not in the manner of dialogue. The missionaries came to implant the Gospel shaped in their own mentality and not to evangelize the people by taking into consideration the people's worldview. The people were not given the chance to enter into dialogue with Christ through his

---

[138] Shorter, *Towards a Theology of Inculturation*, 270.

Gospel. This practice negated the canonical requirements of missionary activities that say:

> By the testimony of their words and of their lives, missionaries are to establish a sincere dialogue with those who do not believe in Christ, so that, taking their native character and culture into account, ways may be opened up by which they can be led to know the good news of the gospel.[139]

The problem persists. However, it must be noted that in places where such a directive is adhered to, the Church and the natives appreciate the practice of inculturation. An example can be seen in the method of Mr. Brown, a missionary who came to Umuofia village:

> Whenever Mr. Brown went to that village he spent long hours with Akunna in his *obi* (seating room) talking through an interpreter about religion. Neither of them succeeded in converting the other but they learned more about their different beliefs . . . In this way Mr. Brown learned a good deal about the religion of the clan and he came to the conclusion that a frontal attack on it would not succeed.[140]

The importance of dialogue as a mean of fostering inculturation can be expressed in the words of Pope John Paul II:

> With regard to African Traditional Religion, a serene and prudent dialogue will be able, on the one hand, to protect Catholics from negative influences which

---

[139] *Canon 787*

[140] Chinua Achebe, *Things Fall Apart.* (New York: Anchor Books, 1959), 179-181

conditions the way of life of many of them and, on the other, to foster the assimilation of positive values such as belief in a Supreme Being who is Eternal, Creator, Provident, and Just Judge, values which are readily harmonized with the content of the faith.[141]

Lack of dialogue is a serious problem that impedes the practice of inculturation, and it has to be urgently addressed if inculturation is to make any head way in Igbo land. We shall discuss more on the process and importance of dialogue between the Church and culture as a way of taking the character and culture of the people into account in sections 4.2 and 5.2 of this work.

---

[141] John Paul II, *The Church in Africa: Post Synodal Exhortation.* "Ecclesia in Africa." (Rome: Vatican Press, 1995), 33.

Chapter Four

INCULTURATING THE CHRISTIAN MESSAGE IN IGBO LAND

4.1 CAN THE CHRISTIAN MESSAGE CO-MINGLE WITH THE IGBO CULTURE?

The Christian message has been looked upon as a divine word that is pure and holy while the Igbo culture and religion has been looked upon as fetish, pagan and impure. With this in mind the questions that arise are, is there a meeting ground between the Message of Christ and the Igbo religion and culture? Can both co-mingle; is it possible to talk of inculturation between the two? To some fundamentalists and "Bible-only" believing Christians, the answers will be no. Such people refer to St. Paul's letter to the Corinthians, which says, "Do not harness yourselves in an uneven team with unbelievers. Virtue is no companion for crime. Light and darkness have nothing in common. Christ is not the ally of Satan, nor has a believer anything to share with an unbeliever. The temple of God has no common ground with idols." (2 Cor. 6:14-18) Here, Christianity and her message is virtue, light, and God's temple while the Igbo religion and culture is represented as evil, darkness, satanic, and temple of idols. This view, however, is very deficient. Christ as we have seen took flesh within the so-called human, evil and dark culture, he grew up in that culture and drew from that culture to communicate his message. Above all the incarnation is the co-mingling of the All-Holy God with 'sinful' humanity. The bible itself came out of a society with its culture and religion; a culture and religion that greatly influenced the language and message of the bible.

The example of Christ himself and the history of Christianity, which was born within the Palestinian culture and developed in the Greco-Roman cultures, strongly suggests that there can be a co-mingling between the message of Christ and Igbo culture; the message of Christ can inculturate in and with Igbo religion and culture. There are many examples from the teachings of Vatican II, the magisterium, the activities of the Church in mission lands and the Igbo experience to support this view.

Encouraging the co-mingling or the inculturation of the Gospel and local customs and traditions, Vatican II teaches that,

> In harmony with the economy of the Incarnation, the young churches, rooted in Christ and built up on the foundation of the Apostles, take to themselves in a wonderful exchange all the riches of the nations which were given to Christ as an inheritance (cf. Ps. 2:8). They borrow from the customs and traditions of their people, from their wisdom and their learning, from their arts and disciplines, all those things which can contribute to the glory of their Creator, or enhance the grace of their Savior, or dispose Christian life the way it should be.[142]

Furthermore, the council reaffirmed this stand in the *Pastoral Constitution of the Church in the Modern World* by stating that,

> The Church, sent to all peoples of every time and place, is not bound exclusively and indissolubly to any race or nation, any particular way of life or any customary way of life, ancient or modern. Faithful to her own tradition and at the

---

[142] *Ad Gentes*, n. 22.

same time conscious of her universal mission, she can enter into communion with the various forms of culture, to their enrichment and the enrichment of the Church herself.[143]

A very good example on the reality of the co-mingling of the Christian message and Igbo culture is the address of Pope John Paul II to the Nigerian Bishops (the majority of whom are Igbos), on February 15, 1982 in Lagos, Nigeria:

> An important aspect of your own evangelizing role is the whole dimension of the inculturation of the Gospel into the lives of your people. Here, you and your priests co-workers offer to your people a perennial message of divine revelation . . . you help them to bring forth from their own living traditions original expressions of Christian life, celebration and thought. The Church truly respects the culture of each people . . . She does not intend to destroy or to abolish what is good and beautiful." [144]

The Christian message does not take root in a vacuum; grace builds upon nature. So also for the Christian message to take root in the lives of the Igbo people, it must co-mingle with the culture of the people, which is their way of life. It should not isolate the Igbo culture but should feel at home in it through the process of dialogue and inculturation. In the process of co-mingling and interacting with the Christian message, Igbo culture, will "constantly re-examine and continuously redefine itself."[145]

---

[143] *Gaudium et Spes*, n.58

[144] John Paul II, "Message to the Catholic Bishops of Nigeria", on February 15, 1982 in Lagos, in *The Popes Speaks on African Traditional Religion and Cultural Values*. http://www.afrikaworld. net/afrel/atr-popes.htm (accessed May 25, 2008).

[145] Chibueze Udeani, *Inculturation as Dialogue: Igbo Culture and the Message of Christ.* (Amsterdam: Rodopi, 2007), viii.

Another perfect example of this co-mingling of the Christian message and Igbo culture is seen in Chinua Achebe's *Arrow of God*. Here, Moses Unachukwu, a catechist and one of the first converts in the Umuaro community, found ways to accommodate Christianity to the local environment and to advance its popularity. Acting without the knowledge of his zealous missionary supervisors, Moses put a stop to the Christian attack on a sacred python cult, much to the relief of the natives. Later, he figured out how to incorporate the annual cultural yam festival within the Christian worship service. This blending of Christianity and traditional religion enabled the Church to take away some of the traditional priest's power and to win over new converts over to Christianity, without loosing their identity as Igbos.[146]

What we have seen so far is a clear indication that there are grounds for inculturating the Gospel message in Igbo culture.

4.2 A THOUGHT EXPERIMENT ON THE POSSIBILITIES AND DIFFICULTIES OF INCULTURATING THE CHRISTIAN MESSAGE IN IGBO LAND.

It is no longer an issue whether the Church in Igbo land needs to inculturate in and with the religion and culture of the Igbo people. The Vatican, theologians, scholars and the Igbo people themselves have all considered inculturation as a *conditio sine qua non* for a thorough incarnation of the Christian message in Igbo land. Nevertheless, it should be noted that any inculturation worth the name and exercise should carefully and with open mind analyzes the content of the Christian message with regard to its relevance to the life, experience and situation of the Igbo people. In this case, inculturation will concern itself with such issues as the rites of initiation, family and marriage, rituals and worship, funeral, worldview and the concepts of life, God and society, etc. Currently, the approach of the Church on these

---

[146] Chinua Achebe, *Arrow of God.* (London: Heinemann Education Books, 1964), 45-8.

issues and the way they are celebrated in Igbo land do not seem to address the spiritual and cultural desires of the Igbo people. Considering this, Ndiokwere asked:

> In **Baptism**, does the little sprinkling of water or pouring of few drops of water on the fore-head bring out the full meaning of *washing in the waters* the actual washing away of some "dirt?" In **Confirmation**, does the anointing on the fore-head with a minute drop of Chrism convey the whole idea of receiving the Holy Spirit . . . Is that single external sign sufficient to effect the *initiation into adult Christian life?* . . . To realize the full benefits of the sacraments and to achieve the full integration of Church and culture, it is necessary to explore various ways of making their celebration meaningful to both the receiver and the administrator.[147]

Inculturation must, therefore, cover the areas of liturgy, catechesis, theology, ministries, celebrations of the sacraments, and para-liturgical celebrations. In this exercise, the words of Cardinal Francis Arinze (a Nigerian-Igbo Cardinal) should be at the back of one's mind:

> Inculturation should be compatible with the Christian message and in communion with the universal Church. Inculturation should not make a 'village church' or a 'national church'. It should make part of a Church, which is universal but also local. It is a caricature of inculturation to understand it as the invention of the imagination of some enthusiastic priest, who concocts an ideal on Saturday night and tries it on the innocent

---

147 Nathaniel I. Ndiokwere, *The African Church, Today and Tomorrow,* vol. II. (Enugu: Snaap Press, 1994), 99.

congregation the following morning. He may have good
will, but good will is not enough.[148]

Following the words of Cardinal Arinze, it is good to note that
our discussions regarding the practice of inculturation and what to
inculturate are only thought experiment. They are subject to the
examination and approval of competent ecclesiastical authorities,
namely the local ordinaries, (Bishops) and their representatives who
are charged with the pastoral life of the people of God within their
respective dioceses. The bishops, in this regard will not act only
unilaterally, maintaining relationship with the Vatican, but also
bilaterally, consulting, interacting and dialoging with the natives
and all those concerned within such local Churches in Igbo land.
With this, the authorities will avoid what can be seen as western
imperialism in the practice of inculturation.

Our thought experiment on the possibilities and dangers or
difficulties of inculturating the Christian message in Igbo land
will be limited to the following areas: Baptism and Confirmation
vs. Igbo initiation ceremonies, Church marriage vs. Traditional
marriage, the Cult of the Saints vs. Ancestral veneration, and
Christian celebrations vs. Igbo music and dance.

**i.) Baptism and Confirmation versus Igbo initiation
ceremonies.** The sacraments of baptism and confirmation
have been called sacraments of initiation. In these sacraments,
the initiates become members of the Church and matured in
the faith, until then, no matter how 'active' one may be in the
Church, he/she remains 'an outsider'. Accordingly, "Baptism
is a Sacrament which cleanses us from Original Sin, makes us
Christians, children of God, members of the Church and heirs of
Heaven . . . Confirmation is a Sacrament by which we receive the
Holy Ghost, in order to make us strong and perfect Christians and

---

[148] Arinze on inculturation on liturgy vs. 'Reverend Showman' in
Catholic Online Forum http://forum.catholic.org/viewtopic.
php?f=158&t=48875&start=... (accessed May 27, 2008)

soldiers of Jesus."[149] Both sacraments may be celebrated on the same day, but in most cases, they are done differently. Baptism opens the door, makes the person a member of the Church while confirmations at a latter time completes the journey making the person an adult member of the Church with full rights and benefits.

On the other hand, in Igbo land inclusion or entrance into the family and community happens through a process of initiations from birth to adulthood. Without these rites of initiation, one is not considered a member of the society. This is typical of all African societies. Reporting on this Mbiti said, "Nature brings the child into the world, but society creates the child into a social being, a corporate person. For it is the Community which must protect the child, feed it, bring it up."[150] These rites start with the naming ceremony. The names are given depending on the circumstance of the birth, but generally in the connection with the ancestors. Before the name is given, the child is simply called *nwa muo* (child of the spirits). In the giving of the name the spirit of the ancestor and the community are brought together. As Magesa noted, "Africans relate to the ancestors through naming: We tend to see them again in the physical features of the children who bear names, which relates stories about their deeds and achievements."[151] Before the baby takes the name, the mother "takes a bath and the baby is washed with the medicinal water, a symbolic act marking the end of one phase of life, and the beginning of a new one."[152]

The naming ceremony begins the rite of initiation into the Igbo society just as the giving of a name begins the rite of

---

[149] Francis Ripley, *This is the Faith*. (Illinois: Tan Books, 2002), 225,236.

[150] John S. Mbiti, *African Religions and Philosophy,* 2ⁿᵈ ed. (Ibadan: Heinemann Books, 1969), 107.

[151] Laurenti Magesa, *Anatomy of Inculturation: Transforming the Church in Africa.* (New York: Orbis Books, 2004), 21-22.

[152] Mbiti, *African Religions and Philosophy,* 116.

Christian initiation—Baptism. Continuing on what follows after, Mbiti said:

> When the Child is still small other rites are performed which are considered necessary before the child can be a full member of the society . . . It is known as 'second birth' or 'to be born twice.' This takes place before the child is initiated [into full adulthood]; unless the child has gone through this 'second birth,' he cannot participate fully in the life of the community. He is forbidden to assist in the burial of his own father, to be initiated, to get married, to inherit property and to take part in any ritual . . . The rites of birth and childhood introduce the child to the corporate community, but this is only the introduction. The child is passive and he must grow out of his childhood and enter into adulthood physically, socially and religiously. This is a change from passive to active membership in the community.[153]

From the above quotation, we can call the 'second birth' baptism, which begins with the naming ceremony, and the full initiation into adulthood, we call confirmation. Just as without baptism one is not considered a Christian so also one is not considered a member of the Igbo community without the 'second birth'. Again, just as without confirmation, one is not an adult Christian, so one is not an adult member of the Igbo community without the full rite of initiation.

The big question here is, what happens when one is baptized and confirmed as a Christian without the traditional native rites? The answer is obvious. One is cut off from one's relatives and community, and for the true Igbo that is equal to death. This has been the situation in most Igbo communities where the traditional rites are seen as unchristian and must not be participated in by

---

[153]   Ibid, 112-113,117.

Christians. In this situation, the Christian finds himself in a divided loyalty between his Church and his culture.

To remedy this situation, the Christian rites of initiation should inculturate with the Igbo rites of initiation. As a thought experiment, I propose that for those families who are already Christians, the traditional naming ceremony and the 'second birth' should be combined together with Church baptism. This ceremony can be performed in the village hall or Church building in the same village. It should not be performed outside the village because; the candidate must be incorporated into his own particular village, in the presence of both community and the Church. In the giving of the name, the eldest member of the family, whether Christian or not pronounces the name before the priest. In the invocation of the saints, the names of the child's ancestors are added, as a sign that the child is not only in union with the Church's saints, who are most often foreigners, but also with his own community ancestors. Instead of bathing the baby with the medicinal water from the mother's bath, the Holy water, blessed by the priest, will be used. Here, the water is not sprinkle or poured on the baby's head only as it is being done presently at baptisms; instead, the priest assisted by the eldest member of the family immerses the baby into the water. The clothing of the baby with white cloth by the Church is followed by the rubbing of the child's right hand with the traditional white chalk (*nzu*) by the eldest member of the family. The newly baptized/initiated is to be clothed not just with Christian white cloth but also with the traditional cloth of prestige and dignity due to an initiated person. Finally, the prayer and presentation of the newly baptized/initiated into the community and Church is performed first by the elder representing the community and the family, followed by that of the priest who gives the final blessing to all gathered at the ceremony. This celebration is wrapped up with usual traditional/cultural dances and merriment that go with naming ceremony and initiation rites.

As good as this may sound, there are dangers. For example, some over zealous priests or elders might, in the name of inculturation, infused into the celebration many rituals that are essentially unchristian, like animal and blood sacrifices. Instead of being a welcome and wholesome celebration, the whole thing may turn out to be a scandal of faith on both sides. Another danger that may occur is the choice of location. Some very 'traditional' Christians or natives may insist on the village square or hall, while some very 'pious' Christians may insist on the Church as a place of such celebration. This may even lead to physical confrontations by fanatics on both sides.

To address these dangers, there should be a proper catechesis on both sides. Again, the celebration should not be left to the imagination of some enthusiastic priest or elder who concocts an idea at night and tries it out in the morning. There must be a guideline that will specify the rubric that must be followed. This guideline should be a product of dialogue from a committee comprising the members of the Church, the elders of the community, other scholars on both Igbo religion and culture, and the Christian religion and heritage. This committee will resolve the issue of location. They are to specify how and when one location may be preferred to another, because definitely situations may vary from village to village, and from parish to parish.

ii.) Church marriage *vs.* Traditional marriage. This is another aspect of the life of the Igbo Christians where a considerable tension exists between the Christian message and Igbo culture. This area requires inculturation urgently.

The Church teaches that the union of man and woman is truly called marriage only when it is a sacrament. For it to be a sacrament, it must be contracted and celebrated in the Church and in the 'Western European' way. Accordingly, the Code of Canon Law states, "A valid marriage contract cannot exist between baptized persons without its being by that fact a sacrament."[154] Those Christians who are married traditionally without Church marriage are therefore considered by the Church as 'living in sin'

---

[154] *Canon 1055.*

and in 'concubinage'. Persons living in this state are denied full communion with the Church.

They are denied Holy Communion, and in some parishes, their children are not baptized. Above all in the case of death, they are not given full Christian funeral rites.

On the other hand, in Igbo culture church marriage is not traditionally recognized as valid if there are no traditional marriage rites before or after the church marriage. To show the seriousness and importance attached to traditional marriage, Ndiokwere noted that a person who marries only in the Church and not traditionally is "in some extreme cases denied certain rights and privileges in the community and could even be ostracized. It is an obligation and a duty (marrying in accordance with the native custom and tradition) that must be accomplished."[155]

Celebrating both marriages, the Church and the traditional, go with many expenses financially and other wise. As result, most people do one of the two to the risk of either not being a full Christian with all the rights that go with it or not being a full member of one's community. This situation has put many Christians in Igbo land at crossroads.

Addressing this situation to eliminate the dual celebration of marriage with its high cost and dichotomies, Hillary Okeke noted that there is

> Need for a marriage rite that will take into consideration the vision of marriage and culturally rooted marriage rites of Africa in general and Nigeria (Igbo) in particular. The rite will as far as possible eliminate the dichotomy and duplicate of marriage rites so that African/Nigeria (Igbo) Christians can celebrate their marriage in a meaningful culturally relevant ceremony that is compatible with Christian doctrine and discipline.[156]

---

[155] Ndiokwere, *The African Church, Today and Tomorrow,* vol. II, 132.
[156] Ibid., 135.

Following the suggestion of Hillary Okeke (now Catholic Bishop of Nnewi, Nigeria), I propose, as a thought experiment, that the Christian concept of marriage should be inculturated into the Igbo traditional concept of marriage, each drawing from and giving to the other, both maintaining their place of importance to the Christian and the Igbo communities. To achieve this, Church marriage and the traditional marriage can be celebrated together the same day, time and venue to be determined by both families and the parish priest. As a norm, I will suggest the groom's village or compound square, which according to Ihechiowa custom is the proper place for the celebration of marriage according to native laws and customs. Again, I am suggesting this place instead of the Church because Canon law does not stipulate that a valid and licit marriage must be celebrated only in the Church.

During the celebration, responsibilities are shared between the elders and the priest. An elder or the bride's father performs the strictly traditional aspect like the giving of wine as custom demands. The priest does the receiving and exchange of consent as well as the blessing of rings and the nuptial blessing. The celebration may go like this: the bride collects a cup of palm wine from her father or an elder acting in his capacity, searches and finds her groom who receives the wine and drinks. Both will go back to the bride's father together with his (groom's) father who blesses his daughter and gives her to the groom's father who receives the bride and hands her over to his son with a blessing. Together both families will now present the couple to the priest who welcomes them in the name of the Church, and asks and receives their consent. The movement of the families to the priest is to be accompanied by a traditional wedding dance. The dress code should be strictly native and traditional for the couple and elders, who confirm the traditional effect of the marriage, and clerical for the priest who confirms the Christian and the sacramental effect of the marriage celebration.

One major difficulty or danger of inculturating the Christian marriage and the Igbo traditional marriage is that there are certain aspects of the Church's theology of marriage that do not go down well with the Igbo concept of marriage. Such aspects include monogamy versus polygamy, the issue of unity and indissolubility of marriage and the problem of childlessness. For example, Catholic theology teaches one man one wife. The Igbo culture on the other hand favors a man to marry as many wives as he can maintain. Again, unlike Christian marriage, Igbo marriage allows for divorce for any reason whatsoever, including childlessness or the birth of only female children.

To address this danger, there should be flexibility in the teachings of the Church, taking into consideration the multi nature of the world. For example, the theology of one-man one wife may work well in most European and American nations based on their cultures and state laws. In Nigeria and Igbo land, the Church should adjust her theology to reflect the culture and the state law that favors polygamy. Monogamy in Igbo land should be a matter of choice and not a matter of Church law. Again, to overcome the problem of childlessness as an obstacle to inculturation, the Church should understand the worldview of the Igbo people. In Igbo land, it is the child, especially, the male child that continues the family lineage. A man without a child is a good as dead. Therefore, the Church should give concession for a polygamous marriage, in unions that produce offspring. Actually, the Vatican and the local ordinary have given such concession to a few individuals in Igbo land. Nevertheless, to overcome this danger completely, such concession should not be limited to only privileged people. It should become a norm.

On the other hand, the Church should educate the Igbo culture to appreciate and respect the dignity of the female child, given the fact that women today, not just in Igbo land but world over, are competing favorably with their male counterparts in every field of life. When the dangers mentioned above are addressed, the Igbo people will accept any rite or celebration of marriage, be it in the Church or in the groom's or bride's compound, as this in not really a problem in Igbo land.

iii.) The Cult of the Saints *vs.* Veneration of the Ancestors. One of the accusations against the Igbo culture and religion, and indeed African traditional religion as a whole by the white missionaries was the worship of ancestors. However, does Igbos worship the ancestors? The answer could be yes or no, depending on the distinction one makes between worship and veneration. The Igbos venerate (respect and honor) the ancestors by maintaining ritual and cultic relationships with them. The same relationship that is found in the cult and communion of the saints in Christianity, and which is defined as veneration not worship, is what obtains in Igbo culture in relation to the ancestors. The food and other sacrificial objects offered to the ancestors were and still often are ridiculed by missionaries and Christians while in fact they (the missionaries and Christians) are guilty of the same 'offence'. Bolaji Idowu recalled a very interesting example:

> We call to mind here the popular story about the Englishman who went to place a wreath on the tomb of a deceased relative at the same that a Chinese was putting rice on the tomb of his own deceased relative: the Englishman characteristically asked the Chinese, 'My friend, when is your relative going to eat that rice you are offering?' To which the Chinese promptly replied, 'When yours is smelling your flowers!'[157]

The Igbo people, like other African tribes, have a strong belief in the ancestors who still 'live among them'. They are given place of honor in every traditional celebration. They are invoked both in formal and informal prayers. They are invoked spontaneously to come to the rescue of their people when things go wrong. They are asked to guide and protect the living, just as the Catholics invoke and ask the intercession of the saints.

Ancestral lineage is also part of Christianity. Jesus came into the world through an ancestral lineage. The gospel of Matthew

---

[157] E. Bolaji Idowu, *African Traditional Religion: A Definition.* (New York: Orbis Books, 1975), 179.

1: 1-18, records a total 42 ancestral generations between Jesus and Abraham. Jesus is called the son of David because of this ancestral lineage.

In Christianity also, especially in Catholicism, the cult of saints who are our ancestors in the faith is very powerful. In addition to honoring and venerating individual saints, the Church marked out November 1 every year as All Saints day celebration, a day that the communion of saints—the saints in heaven, on earth, and in purgatory, is observed. On November 2 in most dioceses in Igbo land, masses are celebrated in cemeteries to remember and to pray for the dead.

In the spirit of inculturation, the Igbo ancestors, baptized or not, should be included in the canon of the mass, especially in the Eucharistic Prayer 1 that has a list of saints who are in communion with the Church. Igbo ancestors should be included in the Church's litany of saints recited during solemn occasions. Images of Igbo ancestors, especially those who sacrificed their lands and resources to build Churches in Igbo land, and those who are known to have been examples of truth and justice should be kept in Churches in Igbo land. This will make the Igbos feel at home in the Church in the sense of being at home and in communion not only with the saints they never knew or saw, but with their own ancestors that they knew, saw, lived with, and whose examples and legacy they will willingly emulate. When this is done, the people will no longer see the Christian liturgy as a performance of the white man's drama, but a celebration that involves them and their ancestors.

One of the dangers that may occur in the inculturation of the cult of the saints and veneration of the Igbo ancestors is idolatry. Some people may not be able to draw the line between worship and veneration. They will go as far as idolizing their family ancestors and worship them as deities. Some may even build local shrines in their graves. Another danger may occur during the funerals of would be ancestors. In Igbo culture, there is an elaborate funeral rite for some one who lived well and died at a ripe old age. These rites include sacrificing to the native gods, and being buried with human heads in some parts of Igbo land.

To avoid these dangers, there should be a proper catechesis on the difference between worship and veneration. There should not also be a regulation forbidding any Christian to set up an altar in the graves of the deceased nor should they pour libations as the pagans do in the process of invoking their intercession. It is enough to mention their names as in the same manner that Christian saints are mentioned during liturgical celebrations. During funerals, the parish priest or his representatives should be at the home of the deceased when the coffin is closed and should not leave the grave side until everything is over to makes sure that no other sacrifice is performed and no human head or any other object is buried in the grave.

iv.) Christian celebrations *vs.* Igbo music and dance. Music and dance are part of Igbo culture and religion. There are music and dance for everything, be they joyful or mournful celebrations. According to Schineller, in Igbo land

> A celebration without song and dance, without a deliberate, unrushed atmosphere, is no celebration at all. When Nigerians gather to celebrate, as they frequently do, the occasion is most often marked by joy and festivity. Traditional dances with traditional costumes link the person with the past.[158]

On the contrary, the Christian liturgical celebrations, especially in the orthodox missionary Churches, are dull, dry and very formal. In most dioceses and parishes, bishops and priests forbid dancing and clapping during liturgical celebrations. The Igbos who are used to singing, drumming and dancing do not feel spiritually satisfied after attending such celebrations. As a result, they resort

---

[158] Peter Schineller, *A Handbook on Inculturation.* (New York: Paulist Press, 1990), 77.

to traditional ceremonies and African Indigenous Churches where they can freely express their joys and emotions through dancing, singing and clapping. Observing this phenomenon, Magesa noted, "Worshippers get bored in our churches mainly because they are not helped to participate meaningfully in the worship"[159] through music and dancing.

To make the Christian message more meaningful and appealing to the Igbo people, there is need to inculturate all the Church celebration with traditional music and dance. On this point, I agree with Ndiokwere that:

> Instead of the colonial and foreign melodies of Bach and Handel and the Gregorian chant, Igbo should bring their traditional local instruments and hymns into the liturgy to make it more lively and enjoyable. Singing, drumming, dancing, taken together should form the central part of Church public worship in Igbo land.[160]

Such music and sacred dances can be part of the entrance, offertory and dismissal procession during the celebration of the Holy Eucharist.

One of the dangers that may occur in this regard is the reduction of worship into mere emotional or sentimental expression. There have been cases where people go to some indigenous African churches not necessarily to listen to the preaching of the word of God or to pray, but just to dance. Ask them what the message of the day was, they will not know. There is also the problem that some music and dancing may be unbecoming of the house of God.

To avoid this danger and to effectively inculturate Igbo music and dance into Christian celebrations, liturgical committees should come up with guidelines on when to sing and dance

---

159 Magesa, *Anatomy of Inculturation: Transforming the Church in Africa*, 71.

160 Ndiokwere, *The African Church, Today and Tomorrow, vol. II*, 179.

and the manner of singing and dancing allowed, and when to practice silence in the presence of God. The whole celebration should not be just singing and dancing. In as much as worship without external manifestations of emotion does not fit in within the Igbo culture, it must be noted that worship without silence and internalization of what is celebrated in not complete. There must be a proper blending of both.

Above all, the general danger that may occur in the implementation of the above thought experiments is what I may call the Igbonization of the Church. In order to enjoy the autonomy granted by the Vatican to inculturate into the life of the Church whatever that is good and wholesome in Igbo culture as a way of making the Christian message relevant in the lives of the people, the Igbo church may turn into a form of church that is completely new and without connection with the universal Church. To avoid this, the Igbo Church and Christians must remember that the aim of inculturation is not to form an independent local Church that is not part of the universal Church in her ministry and worship. Hence, to avoid aberrations there should be a periodic check by the local ordinaries, directly or indirectly through the liturgical commissions, in collaboration with non-Christian elders, on the activities of the priests and parishioners in the local parishes and villages. These commissions would call the erring priests or parishioners to order, as well as recommend appropriate sanctions when and where necessary.

4.3 THE GOALS OF INCULTURATING THE CHRISTIAN MESSAGE IN IGBO LAND.

Inculturating the Christian message in Igbo land has multiple goals ranging from making the Church a truly local Church where the Igbos can be at home to worship in ways familiar to them to effective and grassroots evangelization in Igbo land.

One of the major goals of inculturating the Christian message in Igbo land is for the Church to truly take flesh in Igbo culture. In this truly incarnate Church, the people will live their faith more integrally as Igbo people. Expressing this belief, Udeani said:

Inculturation has the goal of making it possible for Africans to be Africans and remain Africans even after they have become Christian. It will enable the Message of Christ to act as a catalyst in African culture . . . In a way it is concerned with presenting the Message of Christ in a particular African context within the universal church.[161]

What this means in practice is that the Igbo people, as truly Africans, will no longer feel guilty to express the truth about Jesus using symbols, images and rituals immediately available to their heart, intellect and understanding, and without receiving the damnation of the Church as pagans and anti-Christians.

Another aim of inculturating the Christian message into Igbo culture as is to make the liturgy more lively and meaningful to the Igbo Christians. This will create a better appreciation of the Christian mysteries by translating and celebrating them manners familiar to the people. As Pope John Paul II noted, the goal of this exercise is:

To lead them (Igbos) to a better understanding of the mystery of Christ, which is to be lived in the noble, concrete and daily experiences of the African life. There is no question of adulterating the word of God, or of emptying the Cross of its power (cf. 1 Cor. 1:17), but rather of bringing Christ into the very center of African life and of lifting up all African life to Christ. Thus, not only is Christianity relevant to Africa, but Christ, in the members of his Body, is himself African.[162]

---

[161] Udeani, *Inculturation as Dialogue*, 196-7.

[162] John Paul II, "Message to the Catholic Bishops of Kenya", on May 15, 1980 in Nairobi, in *The Popes Speaks on African Traditional Religion and Cultural Values*. http://www.afrikaworld.net/afrel/atr-popes.htm (accessed May 28, 2008).

Inculturation will also promote the spreading of the Christian message in Igbo land. It will help the Church to be rooted in the people's culture, and the Igbos will become at home with the Christian teachings, rituals and celebrations that are now expressed in ways familiar to them. This will help the Church to avoid the mistake of the past, as there are places that the Church did not survive for lack of inculturation. For example, the first attempt by the Portuguese missionaries to evangelize the Igbo people in the 16th century was a failure because the Church did not take root in the people's life and culture. As soon as the missionaries left the shores of Igbo land, the people went back to their native religion, as Christianity was too foreign to them. [163] The Church should learn from history.

The whole exercise of inculturation is to make Jesus present to every one according to their cultural expression. It is to make the 'old' Christian message ever young and new, and appealing to Igbo people of all ages. In this exercise, the Church's theology and catechesis will reflect and address the people's inner longing and worldview. Paraphrasing the words of Leonardo Boff, through inculturation Jesus Christ adopts new forms and new approaches in carrying out his saving mission to the world, the Gospel acquires a new cultural language and the Church is thereby enriched. Every sector of the Christian life is affected. Theology is reformulated. Religious education renders explicit the dialogue between Christ and the local culture. The liturgy gives cultural expression to the people's faith. The universal hierarchical structures of the Church are not replaced, but since they operate in the service of the Christian community, their functions acquire new tasks in the dialogue with culture.[164] In this process of inculturating the Christian message in Igbo

---

[163] A.G. Nwedo, *Christianity Among Us, Its Continued Survival*. (Aba: Nigerian Printer Publications, 1990), 5.

[164] Leonardo Boff, *Ecclesiogenesis: The Base Communities Reinvent the Church*. (New York: Orbis Books, 1986), 24.

culture, the universal hierarchical structures of the Church are not replaced because, in Igbo society, religion and culture are also hierarchically structured. There are high priests, ordinary priests and priestesses, and council of elders called *Ndi Ichie* in the Igbo religious culture and society.

Chapter Five

THE PROSPECT AND CHALLENGES OF INCULTURATING THE CHRISTIAN MESSAGE IN IGBO LAND

5.1 PROSPECT AND CHALLENGES.

Pope John Paul II rightly described the African Church as the future and hope of the Church. Coming into Africa, this future and hope lies in the Nigerian Church, and coming closer home to Nigeria, it rests primarily on the Igbo Church that houses the only Basilica in Nigeria and is the home of the first and only beatified Nigerian in the person of Blessed Michael Iwene Tansi. Presently, the number of priestly and religious vocations, and the number of the faithful in Igbo land are increasing substantially. To sustain this tempo and avoid the mistake of the past, inculturation must be given priority of attention. There are already indications of the willingness of the people to incorporate the Christian message and practices into their cultural ways of life. All these confront the hierarchy and the lay faithful in Igbo land with a lot of challenges.

One of the greatest challenges is to find possible ways of making the theology, the doctrine, and the catechesis of the

Church more relevant to address the people's lives, experiences and situations not just as Christians but as Igbos. In doing this, the message of Christ will not only bring joy and solace to those who are already Christians but will also appeal to and attract non-Christians. The question asked by Schineller regarding the Church catechesis and Nigerian-Igbo culture readily comes to mind.

> The numbers of young children attending catechism classes faithfully throughout Nigeria is astounding . . . And this will continue to be the case. But what catechisms are being used? Do they reflect African ways of thinking and learning, or are they simply imported from Europe and America? Should there be more inclusion of proverbs and stories in catechesis, both of which feature prominently in African life as well as in the ministry of Jesus?[165]

To the question whether the catechisms reflect Igbo ways of thinking and learning, the answer is no, and whether they are imported from Europe and America, the answer is yes. As for whether there should be an inclusion of African, and in particular, Igbo proverbs and stories in catechesis, the answer is YES. Continuing, Schineller rightly said, "More effort should be given to adult catechesis, so that adults working in schools, marketplaces, and the business world can inculturate Christian values into those spheres."[166] Christians must have the language and skills to share their life experiences as Christians with others in all works of life. The Church is therefore challenged to commit herself to cultural education if she takes inculturation seriously. She must help in giving the people the means of developing their culture. In addition, catechetical

---

[165] Peter Schineller, *A Handbook on Inculturation.* (New York: Paulist Press, 1990)., 84.

[166] Ibid.

programs require syllabi or materials which take cultural themes as the starting-point for each lesson.[167]

Although this task is a task for the whole Church, it falls more heavily on the bishops who are the competent authorities within local Churches. They allow or prohibit experiments in inculturation. They also, after mature reflection in union with the universal Church, effectively promote and harmonize progress in this area,

5.2 CONCLUSION.

We have explored the concept and the practice of inculturation in the life and mission of the Church. In line with the teachings of Vatican II, we have come to appreciate fully that the Church is not enclosed in the Vatican, but has a universal mandate of reaching out to people in their native cultures and traditions. In this, Vatican II tied evangelization together with inculturation.

In order to implement the teachings of Vatican II and meet with the challenges of incarnating the Christian message in Igbo land, it is my recommendation that a working commission on inculturation be established in all the dioceses and parishes in Igbo land. Membership of this commission would be drawn not only from among the Catholic theologians, as has been the case in most place where similar commissions have been set up, but also from followers of traditional religion and culture, and members of other religious and Christian denominations. One of the tasks of this commission would be to study each other's religion in a spirit of openness, and to educate each other on what it means to be a Christian Igbo and an Igbo Christian within an Igbo cultural and religious context. This recommendation is in line with the call made by Cardinal Arinze:

> Each Episcopal Conference should appoint a small group of really competent people who are able and

---

[167] Aylward Shorter, *Towards a Theology of Inculturation*. (New York: Orbis Books, 1997), 262-263.

willing to work on this research in close collaboration
with the Episcopal Conference and, through it, with the
competent Dicasteries of the Apostolic See.[168]

Such groups or commissions, as I have mentioned, should not be
limited to Catholics, but should include experts from Igbo religion
and culture, whether Christian or not. Non-Christians would come
to such commission without any preconceived western ideas of
Christianity.

Let me re-emphasize what I have already said. No true
inculturation can succeed in a spirit of monologue and
imposition of ideas and practices upon people. There must be
an ongoing dialogue between the Church and Igbo people as far
as religion and culture are concerned. As Ikenga Metuh pointed
out, this "dialogue may be expressed in four ways—dialogue of
life, dialogue of deeds, dialogue of specialists, and dialogue of
religious experience."[169] In this exercise respect is very important.
What the Church stands for must be respected and what the
Igbo culture stands for must also be respect.

Finally, I wish to conclude by saying that all that has been
said is only a drop of water in the ocean. Igbo land, its people,
culture and religion, is like a vast land that requires much work,
effort and scholarship. I do hope that if this little contribution is
taken into consideration, the seed of the Gospel planted in Igbo
land in 1885 will grow to a big tree where all Igbo Christians will
feel the joy and grace of being both Christians and Igbos.

---

[168] Francis Arinze, *Pastoral Attention to African Traditional Religion.* .
http://www.afrikaworld.net/afrel/vatican.html (accessed May 30,
2008)

[169] Emefie Ikenga-Metuh, *Dialogue with African Traditional Religion:
The Teaching of the Special Synod on African.* http://www.
afrikaworld.net/afrel/metuh.htm (accessed May 30, 2008)

Bibliography

1. Achebe, Chinua. *Things Fall Apart*. New York: Anchor Books, 1959.
2. Achebe, Chinua. *Arrow of God*. London: Heinemann Educational Books, 1964.
3. Afigbo, Adiele E. *An Outline of Igbo History*. Owerri: Rada, 1986.
4. Arinze, Francis. *Pastoral Attention to African Traditional Religion*. http://www.afrikaworld.net/afrel/vatican.html
5. Arinze on inculturation of liturgy vs. 'Reverend Showman' in *Catholic Online*
6. *Forum*   http://forum.catholic.org/viewtopic. php?f=158&t=48875&start= . . .
7. Bekye, Paul. *African Traditional Religion in Church Documents*. http://www.afrikaworld.net/afrel/atrxadocs.htm
8. Bettenson, Henry. *The Early Christian Fathers*. London: Oxford Univ. Press, 1956.
9. Bettenson, Henry. *The Latter Christian Fathers*. London: Oxford Univ. Press, 1970.
10. Boff, Leonardo. *Ecclesiogenesis: Base Communities Reinvent Church*. New York: Orbis Books, 1986.
11. Bokenkotter, Thomas. *A Concise History of the Catholic Church*. New York: Image Books, 1990.
12. Campbell, Duane E. *Choosing Democracy: A Practical Guide to Multicultural Education, 3rd Ed*. New Jersey: Prentice Hall, 2004.
13. Edeh, Emmanuel M. P. *Towards an Igbo Metaphysics*. Chicago: Loyola Univ. Press, 1985.

14. Eileen, F. and Gloria Thomas. *Living Faith: An Introduction to Theology, 2ⁿᵈ Ed.* Kansas City: Sheed and Ward, 1995.
15. Ejizu, Christopher. *OFO, Igbo Ritual Symbol.* Enugu: Fourth Dimension Publishers Ltd, 1986.
16. Ejizu, Christopher. *The Influence of African Indigeneous Religions on Roman Catholicism, The Igbo Example.* http://www. afrikaworld.net/afrel/ejizu- atrcath.htm
17. *Ekwe Nche Research Institute* http://ekwenche.org/ofo.htm
18. Eze, E. C. "Religion and Philosophy" in *World Era Encyclopedia*, vol. 10, Edited by Pierre-Damien Mvuyekure. New York: Thomas-Gale, 2003 .
19. Flannery, Austin. *Vatican Council II: The Basic Sixteen Documents.* Ireland: Dominican Publications, 1996.
20. Geertz, Clifford. *The Interpretation of Culture.* New York: Basic Books, 1975.
21. Idowu, Bolaji E. *African Traditional Religion: A Definition.* New York: Orbis Books, 1975.
22. Isichie, E. *A History of the Igbo People.* London: Macmillan Press, 1976.
23. John Paul II. *Apostolic Exhortation, Catechese Tradende* . Vatican City: Vatican Press, 1979.
24. John Paul II. *The Church in Africa: Post Synodal Apostolic Exhortation* "Ecclesia in Africa." Rome: Vatican Press, 1995.
25. Küng, Hans. *The Church.* New York: Sheed and Ward, 1967.
26. Küng, Hans. *On Being A Christian.* New York: Image Books, 1984.
27. Leonard, Arthur G. *The Lower Niger and Its Tribe. London*: Frank Cass, 1906.
28. Magesa, Laurenti. *Anatomy of Inculturation: Transforming the Church in Africa.* New York: Orbis Books, 2004.
29. Mbiti, John S. *African Religions and Philosophy 2ⁿᵈ ed.* Ibadan: Heinemann Education Books, 1969.
30. McBrien, Richard P. *Catholicism.* New York: HarperCollins, 1974.
31. Metuh, Ikenga E. *African Religion in Western Conceptual Schemes: The Problem of Interpretation.* Onitsha: Imico, 1991.

32. Metuh, Ikenga E. *Comparative Studies of African Traditional Religions*. Onitsha: Imico, 1987.

33. Metuh, Ikenga E. *Dialogue with African Traditional Religion: The Teaching of the Special Synod on Africa*. http://www.afrikaworld. net/afrel/metuh.htm

34. Ndiokwere, Nathaniel I. *The African Church Today and Tomorrow, vol. I*. Enugu: Snaap Press, 1994.

35. Ndiokwere, Nathaniel I. *The African Church Today and Tomorrow, vol. II*. Enugu: Snaap Press, 1994.

36. Neuner, J. & Jacque Dupuis., Eds. *The Christian Faith: In the Doctrinal Documents of the Catholic Church*. London: Image Books, 1986.

37. *New Advent Catholic Encyclopedia*, http://www.newadvent.org/ cathen/03744a.htm

38. NieBuhr, Richard H. *Christ and Culture*. New York: Harper and Row, Publishers, 1951. Nigerian Tribune, May 18, 2007

39. Nwazue, Onyema. Introduction to the Igbo Language. http:// ilc.igbonet.com/

40. Nwedo, A. G. *Christianity Among Us, Its Continued Survival*. Aba: Nigerian Printer Publications, 1990.

41. Obiego, Cosmas. *African Image of the Ultimate Reality: Analysis of Igbo Idea of Life and Death in Relation to Chukwu*. Berlin: Peter Lang, 1984.

42. Olupona, Jacob K. Ed. *African Traditional Religion in Contemporary Society*. New York: Paragon House, 1991.

43. Onwubiko, Oliver A. *Theory and Practice of Inculturation: An African Perspective*. Enugu: Snaap Press, 1992.

44. Onwubiko, Oliver. *Echoes From the African Synod*. Enugu: Snaap Press, 1994.

45. Paul VI. *Africae Terrarum*, October 29, AAS. Rome: Vatican Press, 1967.

46. Pelikan, Jaroslav. *Jesus Through the Centuries: His Place in the History of Culture*. New Heaven: Yale Univ. Press, 1999.

47. *Popes Speak on African Traditional Religion and Cultural Values*. http://www.afrikaworld.net/afrel/atr-popes.htm

48. Rausch, Thomas R. *Evangelizing America*. New Jersey: Paulist Press, 2004.
49. Ray, Benjamin C. *African Religion: Symbols, Rituals and Community, 2ⁿᵈ Ed.* New Jersey: Prentice Hall, 2000.
50. Reese, William L. *Dictionary of Philosophy and Religion*. New York: Humanity Books, 1999.
51. Ripley, Francis. *This is the Faith*. Illinois: Tan Books, 2002.
52. Robertson, J. M. *Pagan Christs*. New York: Barns & Nobles, 1996.
53. Schineller, Peter. *A Handbook on Inculturation*. New York: Paulist Press, 1990.
54. Shorter, Aylward. *Inculturation of African Religious Values in Christianity—How Far?* http://www.afrikaworld.net/afrel/shorter.htm
55. Shorter, Aylward. *Towards a Theology of Incuturation*. New York: Orbis Books, 1988.
56. *Sunday Tribune*, May 11, 2008.
57. *The Code of Canon Law*. London: Collins Liturgical Publications, 1983.
58. *The Jerusalem Bible*. London: Darton, Longman and Todd, Ltd., 1966.
59. Tylor, E.B. *Primitive Culture*. New York: J.P Putnam & Sons, 1920.
60. Udeani, Chibueze. *Inculturation as Dialogue: Igbo Culture and the Message of Christ (Intercultural Theology and Study of Religion)*. Amsterdam: Rodopi, 2007.
61. Weir, Robert F. Ed. *The Religions of the World: Communities of Faith*. London: Collins Macmillan Publishers, 1982.